ORO FACIAL CLEFT ANOMALIES IN PEDIATRIC DENTISTRY

A CONCISE HANDBOOK

M. PIRAVEEN

Dedicated to my the great lovable father

Late Mr. N.Muthuk Ganesan

Contents

Foreword

It brings me great pleasure to introduce to you the first edition of Dr. M. Piraveen's "ORO FACIAL CLEFT ANOMALIES IN PEDIATRIC DENTISTRY A Concise Handbook". A scientific book requires a lot of writing, modernising and improving such a work to represent a level is more difficult.

I congratulate Dr. Piraveen on completing these tasks effectively. The author's operational abilities and knowledge of paediatric orofacial cleft abnormalities are superbly utilised in this work. He is an excellent student and devoted postgraduate student. The information presented in this edition is highly enriched and covers contemporary ideas in dental orofacial clefts.

Undergraduate and postgraduate students will find the book's engaging, well-illustrated text, simple language, and clear tables and figures to be both entertaining and educational. I always love how the book is illustrated with coloured pictures to make scrolling less strenuous to the eyes. The words used are quite kind and warm.

This book's entire chapter is devoted to discussing cutting-edge, modern methods. The author has placed emphasis on the topic of nasoalveolar moulding especially. This book offers a flawless integration of recent, modern innovations that are also pragmatic and useful. Sincere congratulations go out to the author for all his hard work and effort.

I'm confident that the book will help students develop understanding of the broad topic of paediatric orofacial cleft abnormalities. I'm looking forward to reading many more editions.

Enter Caption

Dr. Virinder Goyal, MDS, MFDS, RCPS (Glasgow)

Member, Board of Directors, International Association of Pediatric Dentistry

Board Member, Pediatric Dentistry Association of Asia,

President, South Asian Association of Pediatric Dentistry,

Past President, Indian Society of Pedodontics & Preventive Dentistry,

Professor & Head, Department of Paediatric & Preventive Dentistry,

Guru Nanak Dev Dental College & Research Institute, Sunam-148028, Punjab, India

Member Faculty of Dental Surgery, Royal College of Physicians and Surgeons, Glasgow

Adjunct Faculty, Dr. D.Y. Patil Dental College, Pune

Fellow, Bangladesh Association of Dentistry International

Acknowledgements

My deepest gratitude goes out to Dr. Naresh Sharma, who served as my guide, for his unwavering support and encouragement. He has served as my study's rock and guided me toward a deeper comprehension of the material.

My deepest admiration goes out to my co-guide Dr. Shveta Sood for her unwavering conviction that nothing is impossibly difficult, as well as for her insightful counsel, frank criticism, and protracted discussions about my work.

Additionally, I want to appreciate my family's crucial contribution. I'd like to express my sincere gratitude to my mother Mrs. M. Raajeswari and late father, Mr. N. Muthuk Ganesan, for their unwavering support, timely encouragement, and unending patience, as well as to my late brother, Mr. M. Suriya Prakash, who served as an example to me and assisted me at every turn in both my personal and academic lives. I owe my family everything since they have yearned for this success.

Dr. Akansha Thapliyal and Dr. Shreyas Shahid, two of my colleagues, have my sincere gratitude for their constant support, belief in me, and provision of all necessary assistance. Thank you from the bottom of my heart to Dr. Megha Sethi, Dr Sabreen Gujral, and Dr Shruti Chopra, who are my seniors, and Dr. Ronika Goyal, Dr Twinkle Chawla, and Dr Tharani Thangaraju, who are my juniors, for always being there without fail. My buddies Dr. Nivedha and Dr. Fazil Ram deserve special appreciation for their unwavering support, generosity, and love.

Last but not least, I prostrate before His Highness in all humility and humanity for having blessed me with everything I have, pardoning my transgressions, and given me endurance and strength through trying times and failures.

CHAPTER ONE

INTRODUCTION

Oro-facial cleft being one of the most common congenital deformities that which has a negative setback on the life of the subject and onto a huge extent has an affect on the associated family due to the collaboration of various environmental as well as genetic factors, this deformity also brings about compromised and reduced quality of life. Proper and efficient treatment of the particular deformity requires a group inclusive of a surgeon specializing in clefts, speech specific therapist, a dental surgeon, a specialist of orthodontics and so forth. Counselling of involved mothers and guardians should be done to ensure that the deformity is addressed at the earliest. More focus on awareness and education on oro-facial clefts should be done, on its preventive measures. Identification of potential risk factors should be prioritised.

"Collectively, these are the most common craniofacial birth defects in humans, affecting approximately 1/800 live births worldwide .OFC are one of the most prevalent birth defects in the United States, with about 20,400 cases born between 1999 and 2001." Low socioeconomic status happens to play a huge part in raising the risk of OFC.OFC generally comprise involvement of the lip, the hard palate or oral cavity's roof and also the soft part of palate. OFC results in consequences comprising of oral, facial and also craniofacial deformity due to the extended involvement of structures in and around the oral cavity.

A cleft lip and palate might effect by having a huge negative brunt on the subject's confidence, societal attributes as well as behaviour especially of the female gender. More often, males are seen to be victimised increasing compare to females corresponding to a ratio of approximately 3:2. It is seen that males account to a higher prevalence of cleft lip occurring isolated or with cleft palate, while on the other hand females are seen to be at a slightly increased risk of occurrence for isolated cleft palate, as mesenchymal of face is acquired through the neural crest. Periconceptional folic acid supplementation can be a significant method to bring about lessening in the incidence of progeny along with oro-facial clefts. It has been observed that zinc is crucial for foetal development and any kind of deficiency of it could lead to occurrence of isolated cleft palate as well as other malformations.

Preventive measures includes slight required modification of parental regime, enhanced and improved diet with incorporation of additional multivitamins and numerous mineral supplements, discontinuation of certain medicines as well as drugs, also increased attentiveness on occupational and social risk factors.

Oro-facial development is a multifaceted process that incorporates the role of various genes and signalling pathways. Changes in any associated one or more than one of the genes involved may potentially lead to the most commonly occurring abnormalities in humans.

OFC is considered an end result of the composite collaboration of environmental as well as associated genetic factors.

"Cell transformation and apoptosis between 14 and 60 days post conception creates the soft and hard tissues of the face from the originating oro-pharyngeal membrane. By 48 days the upper lip is continuous and by 60 days palatal shelf fusion completes facial embryogenesis. Disruption of any of the tightly regulated processes occurring in this time frame by environmental and or genetic abnormalities may then predispose to cleft lip and or palate". Various identified genetic variants of that leading to cleft aetiology are IRF6, MSX1. FGF signalling pathway genes, BMP4 and a locus on 8q but the majority remain inexplicable. Strong interaction between maternal habits of smoking has been seen to contribute to OFC.

Such deformities tend to levy extensive economic and individual health burden, hence requiring significant medical and behavioural interventions.

In both isolated and non-isolated forms of OFC, the part of sub phenotypes have given a huge outlook about the causal factors for it. The non-syndromic or isolated forms of OFC incorporate no other than this kind of developmental or structural damage. The aetiology for such forms of OFC comprise of chromosomal irregularities, conditions involving single gene, environmental experiences and also syndromes of an idiopathic cause.

OFC have seen to have massive impact on that of health, psychosocial as well as economic health, both at personal as well as social levels.

CHAPTER TWO

INCIDENCE AND PREVALENCE

"Worldwide, oral clefts in any form (i.e., cleft lip, cleft lip and palate, or isolated cleft palate) occur in about one in every 700 live births. International estimates that are limited to cleft lip with or without cleft palate range from 7.94 to 9.92 per 10,000 live births. Cleft lip with or without cleft palate is the second most common birth defect in the United States, affecting one in every 940 births and resulting in 4,437 cases every year. Reported prevalence estimates range from 7.75 to 10.63 per 10,000 live births. Isolated cleft palate is less common, presenting in one in every 1574 births."

"The occurrence rate of oro-facial clefts varies by population. Overall, higher rates have been reported in Asians and American Indians (one in 500 births), and lower rates have been reported in African-derived populations (one in 2,500 births; Dixon, Marazita, Beaty, & Murray, 2011). Isolated cleft palate is more frequently found in females than in males, at a ratio of 2:1. In contrast, there is a 2:1 male-to-female ratio for cleft lip with or without cleft palate."

The potentiality of recurrence of a cleft anomaly is dependent on factors that are characteristic in a specific household, including the count of subjects associated with clefts, in what way intimately related they have been, the gender as well as race of the victimised ones and the category of OFC each subject is affected with. Once child with a cleft is born, the potentiality for the subsequent child subject is increased by approximately 2 - 5% (say 2 to 5 probabilities in 100). If by any chance, greater than one affected subject in the associated immediate family, further the risk increases to10-12% (roughly 1 chance in 10). In cases, where it is only the subject who is affected in his or her household, has 2-5% chances that his or her offspring is potential enough to have a cleft deformity. (2 to 5 chances in 100). If the affected, has a close affected known, the risk rises to about 10-12% (roughly 1 in 10). The unaffected siblings of the affected has about 1% (1 in 100) potential of giving rise to an affected offspring. This potentiality increases to 5-6% (5 to 6 chances in 100) if there are more than one affected members. If at all there is any involvement of a syndrome, the potential for recurrence in the same household could rise to about 50% (1 chance in 2).

Based on recent literature, the prevalence of oro-facial clefting is on the upsurge. Through the outstanding enhancements seen in the arena of perinatal care along with prenatal medicinal expertise, it appears probable that added of these fetuses will endure the period and also require treatment.

The congenital prevalence of oro-facial clefts (OFCs) globally has been recognised to vary. However, an efficient evaluation is required. It is of utmost importance to have specific data about wide-reaching OFC congenital occurrence as it may help direct improved comprehension of its causal factors and to cope with public health assets and policies. A systematic work was conducted using electronic databases through portal of PubMed between the years 1950 and June 2015 using specific key words and search terminology of cleft lip palate or oro-facial clefts and that of congenital prevalence or incidence. The birth prevalence rate was articulated by dividing the number of oro facial cleft cases (numerator) by the number of live birth infant (denominator) multiplied by 1,000.

Continent (location)	Numbers of orofacial clefts	Numbers of live births	Birth prevalence (per 1000 live births)	95% confidence interval
Asia	15646	99,65,084	1.57	1.54- 1.60
North America	18,276	11,728,914	1.56	1.53-1.59
Europe	5,028	3,236,253	1.55	1.52-1.58
Oceania	2,822	2,125,912	1.33	1.30-1.36
South America	3,205	3,229,179	0.99	0.96-1.02
Africa	216	380,273	0.57	0.54-0.60
Total	45,193	30,665,615	1.47	1.44-1.50

Table 1. Geographical variation in birth prevalence of orofacial clefts according to continents

Ethnics	Numbers of orofacial clefts	Numbers of live births	Birth prevalence (per 1,000 live births)
American Indians	276	105,366	2.62
Japanese	2,244	1,296,187	1.73
Chinese	8,521	5,476,554	1.56
Whites	22,489	14,494,512	1.55
Blacks	240	410,513	0.58

Table 2. The birth prevalence of Clefts (Lip, Lip and Palate, and Palate) among race

Most of the countries with low socio-economic status lack efficient investigating systems for congenital defects and OFC deformities. Thus, the conveyed birth prevalence rates are not precise according to the WHO International Collaborative Research on some of these regions. Craniofacial Anomalies project including OFC clefts registry is presently commencing surveillance in congenital defects, especially in these countries. The international collaboration for this particular mission is desired.

CHAPTER THREE

EPIDERMIOLOGY

Oro-facial clefts are referred to as syndromic, if at all they are associated with any additional or associated developmental or structural deformities; where as non-syndromic are those if they occur in seclusion without any other associated deformities. "The majority of CLIP cases are Ns (70%). As are about half of CPO cases. The prevalence of OFCs varies from 1/500 to 1/2500 births depending on the geographical origin, racial and ethnic backgrounds, and socioeconomic status".

Differences in birth prevalence leads to huge alterations in the geographical outreach of cleft defects globally. Because of existing lacunae in the record of births and birth defect investigation systems, there is an unclear and incomplete picture. Globally, there is an existing difference in the incidence of anomalies involving that of isolated cleft lip or with cleft palate and also a threefold disparity in the incidence of cleft palate at birth.

There is substantial disparity in the involved share of OFC involved scenarios along with supplementary birth related anomalies as well as syndromes. Presence no account any dependable indication of time trends, nor is there reliable disparity by SES or seasonality, but these regions have not been properly observed. There is a significant necessity to evaluate such parameters inside along with spread along amongst various inhabitants.

There is presence of remarkable global disparity associated in the occurrence of OFCs, but rationality and comparison of data are severely affected by the associated population source, time intermission, technique of determination, inclusion as well as exclusion criteria and also sampling changeability.

There is presence of very limited data involving the prevalence of OFCs associated for various regions around the sphere, comprising regions of Africa and Asia and also that of Eastern Europe. India tends to bare the brunt of craniofacial deformities and anomalies of cleft lip and cleft palate. The country India happens to unfortunately be one of those regions around the globe where documentation protocol for the data including rates of congenital deformities is incomplete. Consistent and wholesome data including figures is tough because of the associated organisation and also because of the involvement of numerous craniofacial abnormalities. It is recognised that in various regions of country India, the invovled parents or guardians of the subject child born along with an associated cleft defect show absence of proper accessibility to counselling based about the maintenance and management. Cleft lip as well as cleft palate might be observed as an intimidating anomaly and there also may be a consciousness about the detail that cleft defects could possibly be corrected using surgical approach along with substantial accomplishment acquired dually from aesthetic as well as functional point of view. The lack of efficient information and proper resources results in undesirable postponements in pursuing and acquiring satisfactory medical care and services, because of which, various new-borns with OFC die due to undernourishment or any residual infection. This particular forbidding situation is additionally intensified by the following

"(a) Failure of healthcare experts to identify craniofacial irregularities as a notifiable condition, and

(b) The World Health Organization (WHO) in their on-going use of the diagnostic classification, other than functional classification of clefts."

The following apparent complications have fortunately being approached recently. Occurrence of variety of ailments attributed to gene related reasons or those which include an element associated genetically to the associated causal factors are recorded.

Disorder	Birth Prevalence	Per year
Congenital malformations	1.00 per 50	490,000
Craniofacial anomalies	1.10 per 1000	26,950
Down syndrome	1.00 per 1139	21,510
Beta-thalassemia	1.00 per 2700	9,074
Sickle cell disease		5,200
Metabolic diseases	1.00 per 2497	9,811

Table 3. Burden of Genetic Diseases at Birth in India

"Calculated at the frequency rate obtained in the 3-center study, and at, 24.5 million births per year. Craniofacial anomalies include cases of CLP and CP. Three multi-centric studies in India provide almost similar frequency of CFAs. Meta-analysis of 25 early studies from 1960 to 1979 involving 407,025 births CL+CP= 440 cases, 1.08 per 1000 births, CP = 95 cases, 0.23 per 1000.

Prospective national study of malformations in 17 centres from all over India from Sept. 1989 to Sept 1990 involving 47,787 births - CL+CP = 64 cases, 1.3 per 1000 births, CP =6 cases, .12 per 1000 births. The latest (1994-1996) three-centres study involving 94,610 births in Baroda, Delhi and Mumbai - frequency of CL+CP 0.93 per 1000, and CP alone 0.17 per 1000."

On the basis of the previous study which was utmost thoroughly directed, count of infants taking birth every year accompanied along with defects of cleft lip and cleft palate accounts to approximately 28,600, which refers to almost 78 number of victimized infants being born on a daily basis or may be 3 no. of. Infants born with cleft defects in every 60 minutes.

Malformation	Rate per 10000	Total no. of year
Neural tube defects	36.3	88,935
Talipes equinovarus	14.5	35,525
Polydactyly	11.6	28,420
Hydrocephalus alone	9.5	23,275
Cleft lip ± cleft palate	9.3	22,785
Congenital heart disease	7.1	17,395
Hypospadias	5.0	12,250
Cleft palate alone	1.7	4,145

Table 4. Estimated Number of Infants with common malformations

Registration of associated defects acquired through birth comprising CranioFacial Abnormalities in country India

It happens to be of significance for a subject with a defect of birth registered here in country India, be it in the form of a pilot oriented study, ideally ought be recognised to accumulate information in numerous centres, on the basis of topographical location, occurrence of lineage as well as area showing high and low incidence illustrated in preceding readings. Associated registration ought to be carried about collaboration along with associated neonatology elements and centres present in various towns which happen to regularly gather data in the targets. In each associated centre, a medical professional along with a social worker might make effort in alliance in analysing as well as accumulating suitable material. Craniofacial abnormalities including that of cleft lip as well as cleft palate defects leads to an accumulation of facts composed along with the protocols incorporated, as this should be those approved.

CHAPTER FOUR

EMBRYOLOGY

DEVELOPMENT OF NEURAL TUBE

All through the third week of embryonic life the neural plate seems to be at the head end of the embryo, this progresses into a midline groove with neural folds on each end which consequently fuses to give rise to a tube. Neural crest cells is derived from the ectoderm, the outer layer of cells of the neural folds which further migrate into the core tissue as mesenchyme and continue the process of migration into the emerging assembly of head and neck where they augment to neural, skeletal and connective tissues.

ESTABLISHMENT OF PRIMITIVE MOUTH

"Throughout the third week, the face is developed as the mouth originates to form. By the time the third week comes to an end, the stomodaeum also known as the primitive mouth has been recognized which is lined by the bucco-pharyngeal membrane. Throughout the fourth week in utero, the buccopharyngeal membrane breaches, thus founding attachment between structures including stomodaeum and the primitive digestive tract. Just before the breach of the membrane, the hypophysis or pituitary gland resumes to form as a small invagination of the stomodeal ectoderm in the roof of the primitive mouth just anterior of the buccopharyngeal membrane.

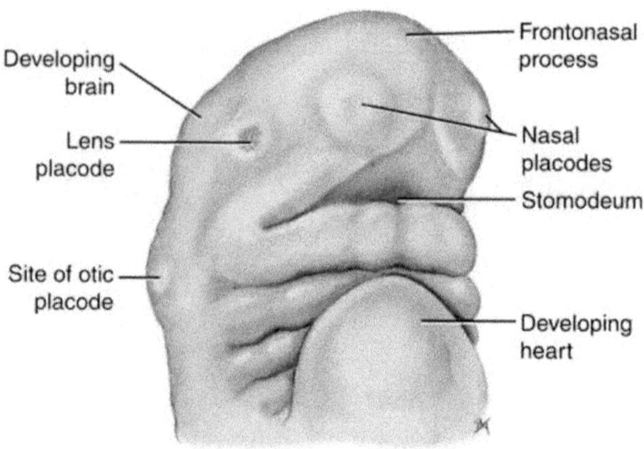

Figure 1: Embryo at the fourth week of prenatal development showing the developing brain, forming face from the growth of the frontonasal process, and developing heart. Note also the placement of the stomodeum and placodes.

The pit moulded by this invagination is referred to as Rathke's pouch. Beyond the stomodeum, the lately developed forebrain gives rise to a huge bulge. The ectoderm and mesenchyme that create this bulge matures into an embryonic structure known as the frontal process, which will further augment to structures involving the upper part of the face, the nasal septum, and the anterior part of the roof of the mouth. Underneath the stomodeum, five paired branchial arches arrange themselves in the region of the future neck. These are customarily labelled as branchial arches I, II, III, IV, and V. Each arch is established chiefly by the migration of neural crest cells from the posterior aspect of the evolving nervous system."

DEVELOPMENT OF FACE

Later, to the formation of the stomodeum, frontal process and branchial arches, the budding of a round process takes place on either side of the first branchial arch. This particular bud is referred to as the maxillary process. It develops in a ventro-medial direction cranial to the chief part recognized as process of mandible. Finally the maxillary processes helps develop the structures including the upper part of the cheeks, the sides of the upper part of lip, and most part of palate. Mandibular processes establishes structures including lower region of the cheeks, lower lip, the lower jaw and region of the tongue.

On each contralateral side of the frontal process, is a compacted area referred to as the nasal placode, ascending from the ectoderm which will ultimately give rise to the nose. Throughout the 5th and 6th weeks the epithelium of the placode invaginates and horseshoe shaped elevations advances around them followed by rapid growth so that the placodes become buried underneath of nasal or olfactory pits. The medial and lateral halves of these elevations are commonly referred to respectively as medial and lateral nasal processes. The part between the two nasal pits, comprising both medial nasal processes is referred to as the fronto-nasal process.

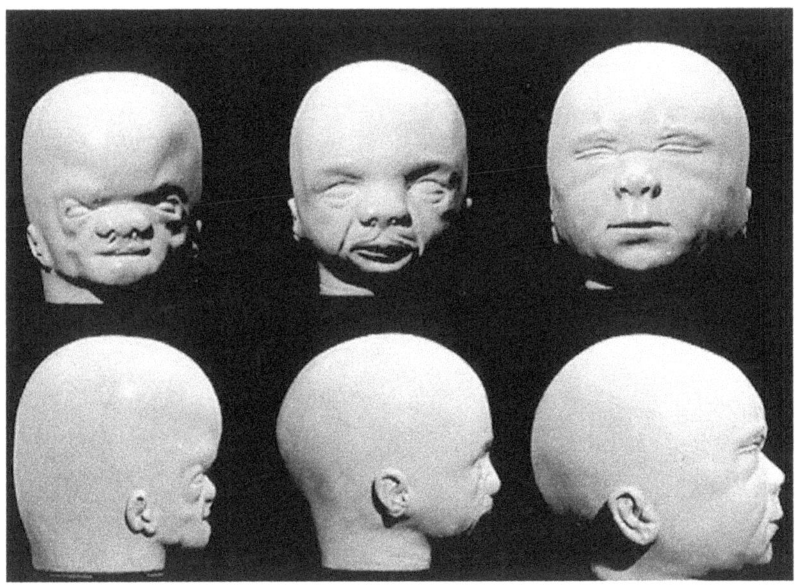

Figure 2: Development of the face

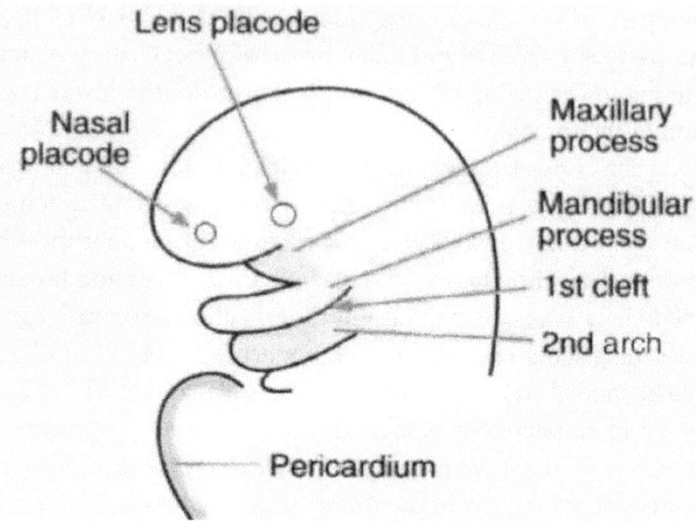

Figure 3: Early stages type I in development of the face seen from lateral side.

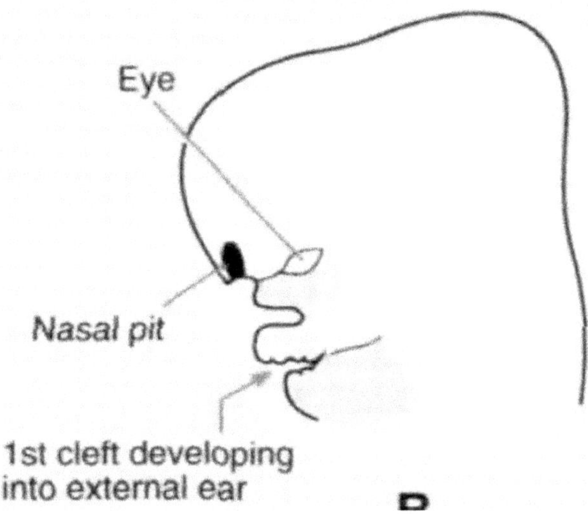

Figure 4: Early stages type II in development of the face seen from lateral side.

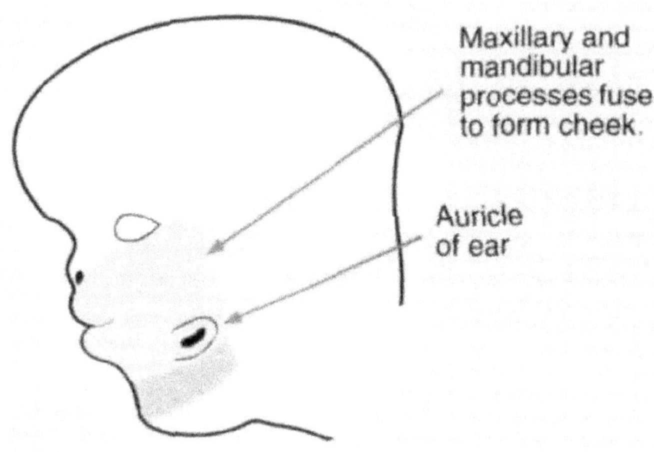

Figure 5: Later stage types I in the development of the face as seen from the lateral aspect.

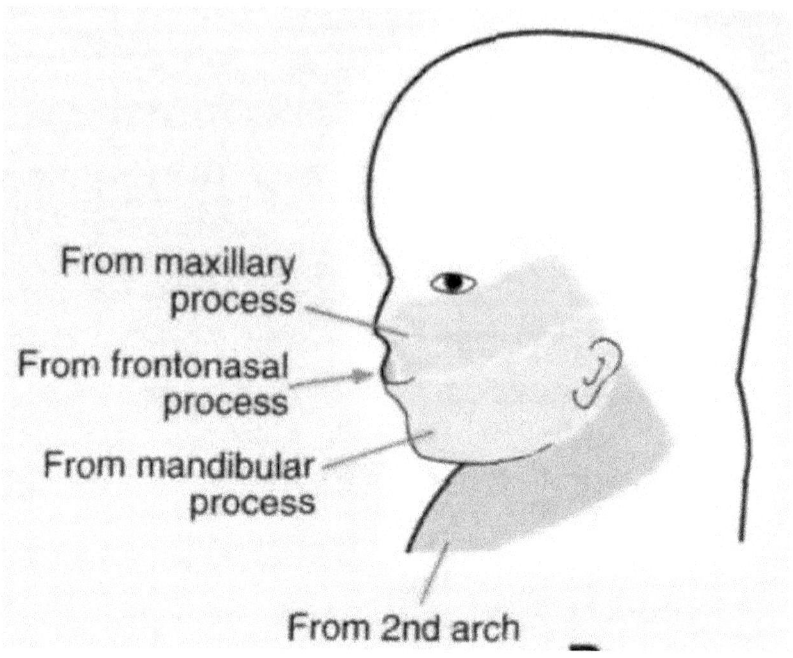

Figure 6: Later stage types II in the development of the face as seen from the lateral aspect.

DEVELOPMENT OF LOWER LIP

Mandibular processes of both the ends develop in the direction of each other and happen to fuse in midline to augment to the lower lip and to the lower jaw.

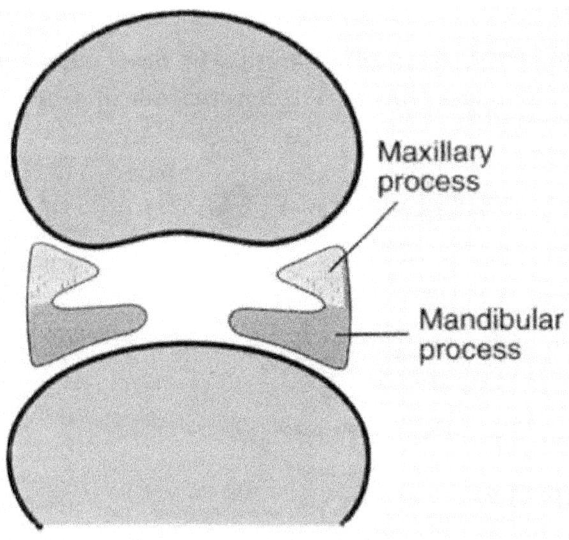

Figure 7: The nasal placode is converted into the nasal pit. Elevations of the pit form the medial and lateral nasal processes.

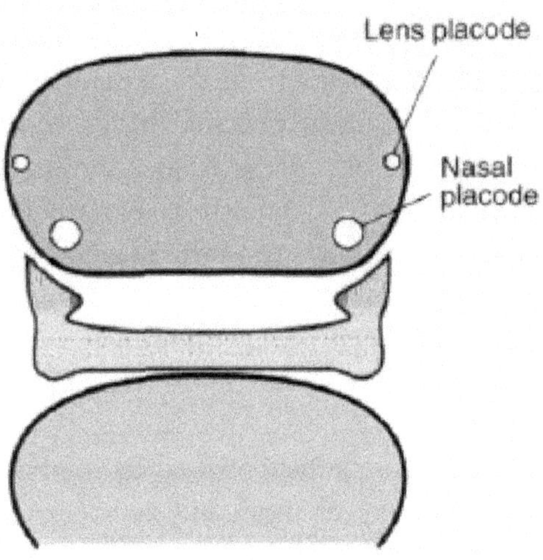

Figure 8: The right and left mandibular processes fuse and form the lower boundary of the future mouth. The nasal placodes appear over the frontonasal process. The lens placode appears.

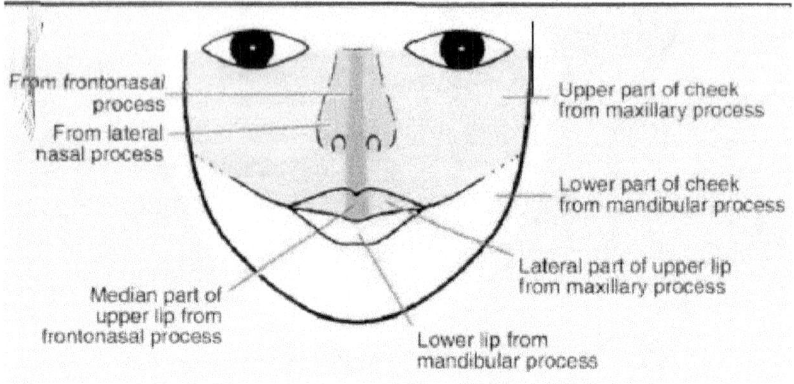

Figure 9: Derivation of parts of the face.

DEVELOPMENT OF UPPER LIP

The maxillary processes develop medially and tend to fuse first and foremost with the lateral nasal process followed by the medial nasal process thus, breaching the nasal pits from the stomodeum. Substantial development of the maxillary process brings about subsequent tapering of the fronto-nasal process. Hence, both the ectodermal and the mesodermal basis of the lateral part of the lip originate from the maxillary process where as the mesodermal process of median part of the lip originate from the fronto-nasal process. The ectoderm of the maxillary process dominates over the mesoderm in order to link with that of the opposite maxillary process in the midline.

A partial or complete failure of a maxillary process to combine with the globular process thus augmenting to a condition referred as cleft lip. Cleft lip may comprise a breach in the amalgamation of the globular process either unilaterally or bilaterally. A cleft lip is obvious by the commencement of the second month in utero, when development of the lip is generally accomplished.

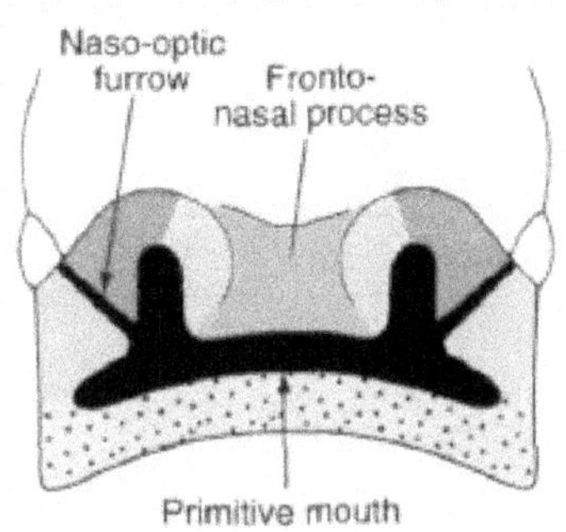

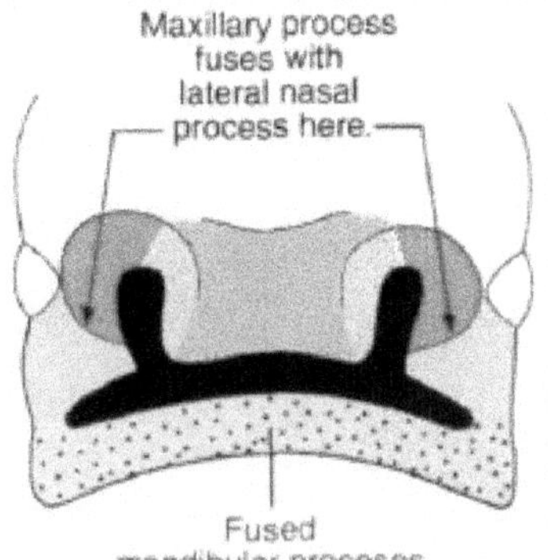

Figure 10: Development of the face (continued).

The right and left nasal pits come close to each other. The lateral nasal process is separated from the maxillary process by the naso-optic furrow.

The maxillary process fuses with the lateral nasal process obliterating the naso-optic furrow.

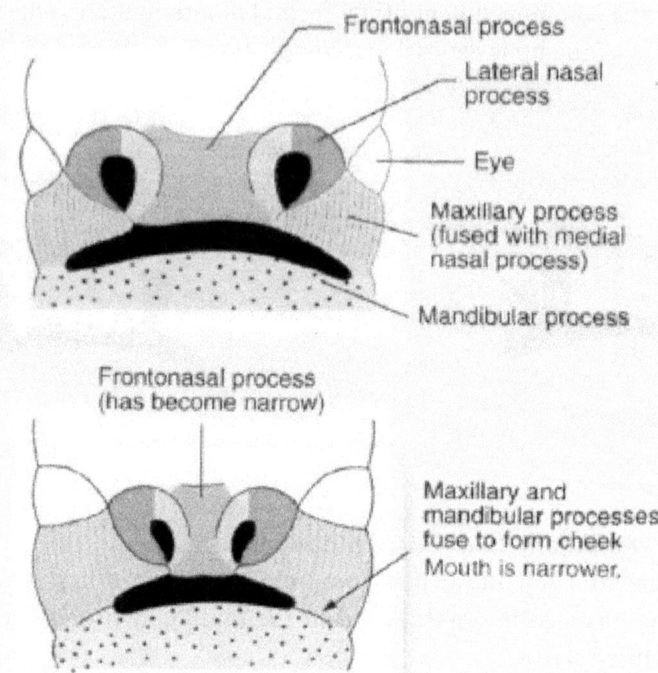

Figure 11: Development of the face

The maxillary process extends below the nasal pit and fuses with the medial nasal process. In this way the nasal pit is separated from the stomatodaeum.

The maxillary and mandibular processes partly fuse to form the cheek. With growth of the maxillary processes the nasal pits come closer to each other.

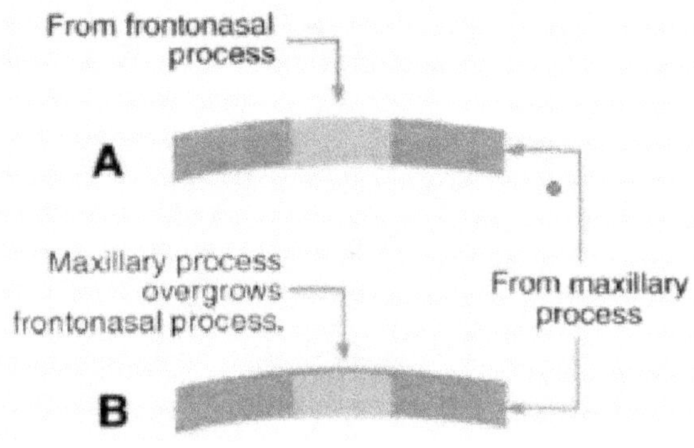

Figure12: Formation of upper lip

DEVELOPMENT OF PALATE

It originates from three sources, including the right and left maxillary processes and the globular process. Within the stomodeum, close to the commencement of the second month, three ingrowths seem to appear. Including, one ingrowth through the internal part of the right side of process of maxilla, an including ingrowth acquired through the internal part of the left side process of maxilla, finally an ingrowth acquired through the internal surface of the associated globular process. These involved ingrowths keen on the part of stomodeum through that of the processes of maxilla are commonly referred to as the corresponding right as well as left lateral processes of the palate. An ingrowth acquired from that of the globular process develops first as a bar of tissue within the stomodeum between and underneath the right and left olfactory pits which further progresses into the pre-maxillary region. The ultimate unification of both the laterally placed processes of the palate with the pre-maxillary region ends the so called Y-shaped opening located at the oral cavity's roof. The element of subsequent alignment of these processes to a changed horizontal position has been the matter of subject of efficient studies. A repeated justification is that, as a consequence of enlargement of the mandible, the tongue tend to drop to the floor of the stomodeum.

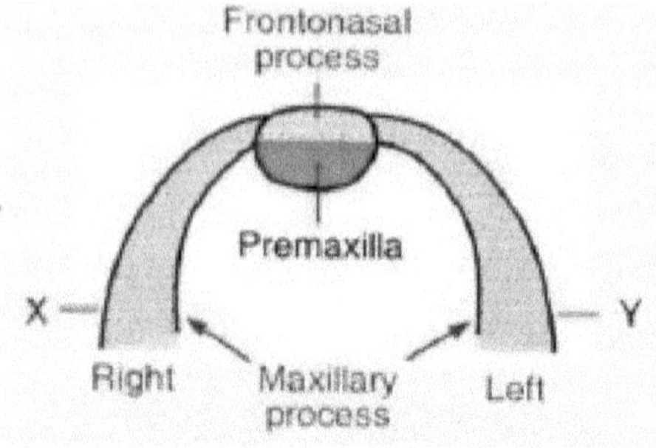

Figure 13: Development of frontonasal process

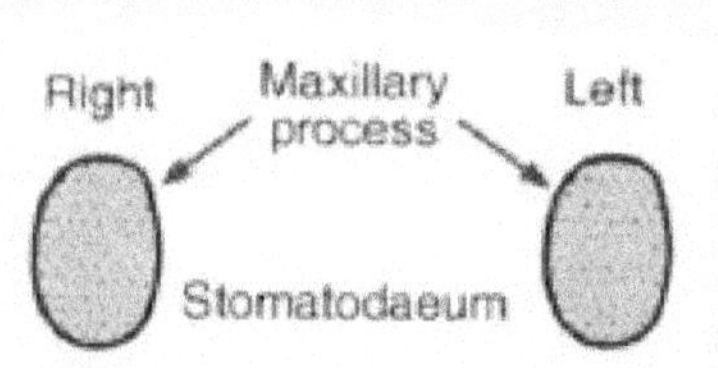

Figure 14: Developing stages of maxillary process

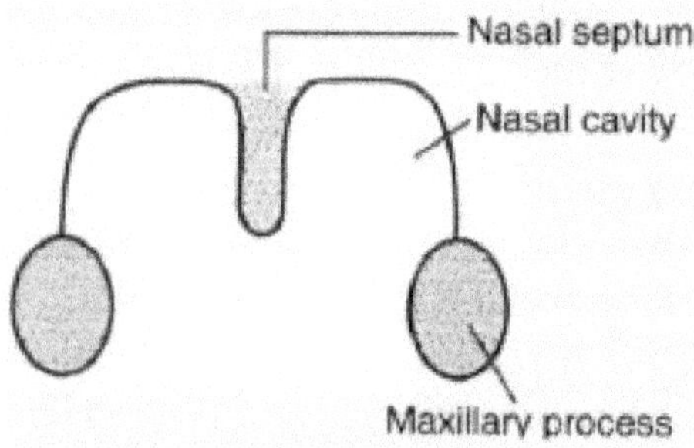

Figure 15: Development of maxillary process

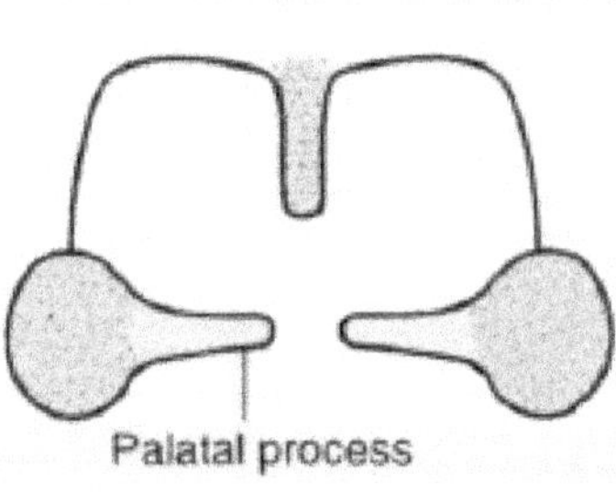

Figure 16: Development of palatal process

When the tongue is thus eliminated from the path of the growing lateral palatine processes, the processes tend to get aligned to a changed horizontal position. After achieving a changed position initially through the third month in utero, the lateral processes of palate tend to develop medially approaching each other and developing pre-maxillary area develops posteriorly. The palatine processes meet at the midline and happen to fuse with each other along with the anterior of the lower border of the nasal septum. Advancing, the happen to undergo fusion with the posterior border of the pre-maxillary growth. The structure developed happens to be present at the roof of the oral cavity and floor of the nasal cavity and the stomodeum gets separated into a lower chamber and an upper chamber, namely.

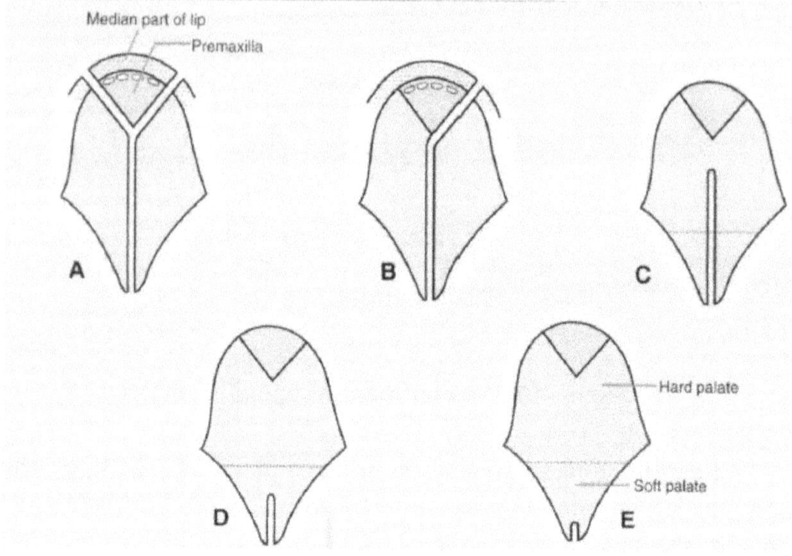

Figure 17: Developing stages of Palate.

When one or both maxillary processes fail to merge with the globular process, it helps originate a cleft of the upper part of the lip, a disappointment of lateral palatine processes in order to undergo fusion along with each other or with that of the pre-maxillary area augmenting to cleft of the palate. Cleft palate is obvious through the commencement of the three month in utero, when the fusion of the palate is generally accomplished. Cleft palate can exist in slight or extensive forms and constrain its involvement only to the uvula, thus not affecting any involved oral function. It may comprise of the soft part of palate, a portion of hard part of palate, or including both soft as well as hard palates. Cleft palate can also occur involving the alveolar ridge unilaterally or bilaterally, showing presence between that of the maxillary lateral incisor and that of the maxillary canine present alongside to the plane of fusion between the pre-maxilla and the lateral palatine process, occasionally the lateral incisor is missing. In cases of severe intraoral clefts, the maxillary teeth may be lacking in number and frequently exist as displaced. Any severe cleft of the palate tends to incorporate a crippling opening amongst the oral and nasal cavities, recognised as a serious brunt to the individual in both processes, that of speaking and eating.

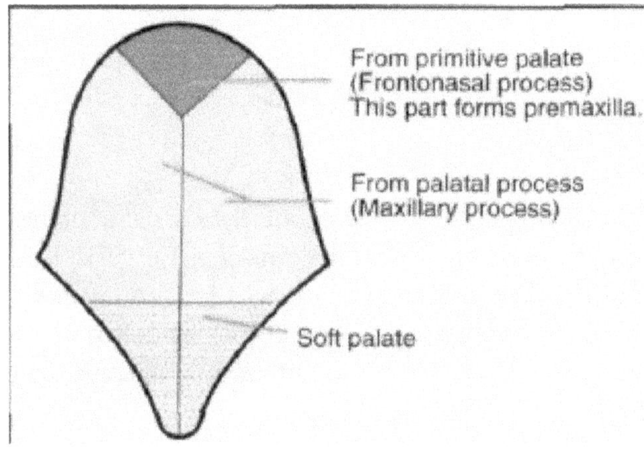

Figure 18: Development of Palate.

CHAPTER FIVE

ETIOLOGY

Orofacial clefting has a polygenic, multi-factorial aetiology that is influenced by both environmental and genetic variables. Despite decades of research, it is still unclear what environmental variables cause the illness and what genes predispose people to it. Candidate gene discovery techniques that are brand-new and cutting-edge are being used.

Oral clefts frequently coexist with a variety of chromosomal abnormalities and syndromes (such as trisomy 13, amniotic band anomalad, Fryns syndrome, Meckel syndrome, Stickler syndrome, Treacher Collins syndrome, van der Woude syndrome, Velo-cardiofacial syndrome, etc.) as well as environmental factors like prenatal medication, maternal alcohol consumption, and smoking. Deficits in nutrition and vitamins, diabetes, pollutants in the environment, altitude, birth order, socioeconomic standing, and parental age. The capacity of the mother to maintain myoinositol and zinc concentrations in red blood cells are additional genetic factors that could influence the occurrence of OFCs (a hexahydroxycyclohexane sugar alcohol). Whenever these nutrients are not correctly digested, mistakes in DNA template and transcription may occur, which is thought to contribute to oral cleft development. Maternal capacity to preserve adequate levels of vitamin B6 and B12 and foetal ability to utilise these nutrients are also considered to play a role in this process.

Amoxicillin, phenytoin, oxprenolol, and thiethylperazine may all have some association with cleft lip or palate (CL/P), whereas carbamazepine and oxytetracycline may all have some organisation with posterior cleft palate (PCP) during in the early stages of pregnancy. Drugs have a small role in the underlying etiology of cleft lip or palate (CL/P). Additionally, it was discovered that moms with both the MTHFR 677TT OR MTHFR 1298CC genotype and inadequate peri-conceptional folate intake had a higher risk of having children with cleft lips with or without palates.

Oral cleft, growth retardations, limbs malformations, as well as other craniofacial deformities are known teratogenic effects of drugs that interfere with the metabolism of folate, such as phenytoin. Oral clefts have been linked to maternal use of vasoactive medications such amphetamine, aspirin, ibuprofen, and pseudoephedrine as well as tobacco smoking.

It has also been shown that anticonvulsant drugs such phenobarbital, trimethadione, valproate, and dilantin raise the risk of cleft lip and palate. Cleft lip and cleft palate can also be brought on by other medications, including Accutane-containing acne treatments and the chemical methotrexate, which is frequently prescribed to treat cancer, arthritis, and psoriasis.

The goal of therapy and surgical repair programmes nowadays is to be as effective as possible in rehabilitating patients and preparing them for a regular social life devoid of prejudice and discrimination. The main control of all craniofacial anomalies needs to be the highest scientific and humanitarian goal. To this purpose, current research focusing on environmental and genetic reasons is in progress. It is primarily focused on (a) features of maternal medical records, lifestyle, and nutrition, and (b) candidate genes.

The procedures used are described in a recent WHO document titled "Global initiatives to minimise the national healthcare burden of craniofacial defects," which aims to coordinate efforts globally and promote global collaborative research.

Rarely does the cleft phenotype spread in a straightforward Mendelian manner, as is the case with many other genetic diseases.

Research of cleft monozygotic reveal a 30 to 60% concordance rate, which supports this. These findings support an important but not only genetic involvement in the growth of cleft lip-cleft palate when compared to the 1.0 to 4.7 percentage concordance rate in dizygotic twins.

If one child in a household has cleft lip-cleft palate, there is a 3–4% probability that what a second child will indeed be born with such a similar problem; if two children have had the disease, there is a 9–% chance that a third child will indeed be born with the defect. Environmental elements like smoke exposure, steroid use, phenytoin use, and retinoids use have all been linked to the growth and development of cleft lip and cleft palate in addition to genetics.

Several factors, including the following, can cause the formation of cleft lip and palate:

1. Genetic influences

Environmental elements

3 connections between genes and environments

Genetic factors

15 percentage of cleft lip-cleft palate instances are syndromic, and cleft lip is a characteristic in 171 syndromes (Table 5). Six are X-linked recessive, while 35 autosomal dominant and 64 autosomal recessive conditions exist. In a study that looked at the correlation between clefting and malformations, malformations were present in 13.6 percent of individuals with cleft lip, 36.8 percentage of patients with the both cleft lip and cleft palate, and 46.7 percentage of patients with cleft palate alone.

Syndrome	Location	Gene
Vander Woude	Iq32-41	
Ectrodactyly ectodermal dysplasia	3q27	*P63*
Margarita Island ectodermal dysplasia	11q23	
Aicardi	Xp22	
Craniofrontonasal dysplasia	Xp22	
Hypertelorism – microtia-clefting	1q, 7p	
Kallman	Xp22	*KALI*
Gorlin	9q22-31	*LMXIB*
Velo-cardio-facial	22q11	

Table 5. Genetic Links to Syndromic Orofacial Clefts

According to reports, five to seven percent of CUP cases are linked to particular disorders. In comparison to dizygotic twin pairs, monozygotic twin pairs have better concordance rates for CLP. Since each defect's family grouping and concord in twins with CLP and CP has now been discovered to be distinct, the flaws are thought to have a variety of etiologies. In CLP prevalence of let-sided clefting, there is a masculine bias. Genetic studies have been carried out in an effort to identify the genes that are involved. These studies suggest a variation of loci, which include regions on x chromosome 1, 2, 4, 6, 9, 14, 17, and 19. A meta-analysis of the whole genome linkage studies also indicates presumed loci at 2q32-q35 and 9q21-q33.

In population-based association studies, a range of gene variations have been examined. TGFa, TGFß3, MSX1, IRF6, TBX22, as well as genes for transcription factors, xenobiotic metabolism (CYP1A1, GSTM1, NAT2), nutrition metabolism (MTHFR, RARA), and immunological response (PVRLI, IRF6), have all been linked to these processes. The MTHFR and TGFa genes have undergone some of the most extensive research over the years. The inconsistent nature of the findings, however, highlights the difficulties in analysing gene-disease relationships and associated interactions.

IRF6, the gene linked to Van der Woude syndrome (VDWS), has been found to play a significant role in the isolated type of clefting. Several other independent investigations in a variety of different cultures and ethnic groups have replicated this conclusion, which is an intriguing recent discovery. The implication is that these genes may contain a mutation that could either cause or modify the expression of the condition. Both these good example of gene 43 variants involved in syndromic forms of CL/P with a mendelian mode of inheritance and generating phenocopies of non-syndromic CL/P are including Kallmann syndrome (FGFR1), ectrodactyly-ectodermal dysplasia/clefting (TP63), X linked ankyloglosis.

A heterogeneous disease entity, non-syndromic cleft lip-cleft palate has putative clefting loci on chromosome 1, 2, 4, 6, 11, 14, 17, and 19. (Table 6).

Gene	Locus
SKI/MTHFR	Ip36
TGFb2	1q41
MSX1	4p16, 1q31, 6p23
PVRL1	11q23
TGFa	2p13
TGFb3	14q24
GABRb3	15q11
RARa	17q21
BCL3	19q13

Table 6. Genetic Links to Nonsyndromic Orofacial Clefts

The non-syndromic oro-facial clefting on chromosome 1 is caused by a mutation in the methylene tetrahydrofolate reductase gene on lq36.

A susceptibility gene for cleft lip and cleft palate has been discovered in the 2p13 area of the short arm of chromosome 2.

The involvement of the MSXI gene on chromosome 4 (4q25), which has been linked to a higher risk of cleft lip-cleft palate, has been the subject of conflicting research. At 6p23 on chromosome 6, there is a gene that likely causes cleft lip and palate.

Chromosome 11, the developing growth factor beta3 locus in chromosome 14, the retinoid receptor genes on chromosome 17, the BCL3 gene, and the translation elongation factors beta locus on chromosome 19 are some other chromosomes that may include clefting sites.

Environmental factors

Environmental variables are increasingly being linked to oro-facial clefting. Environmental risk factors include maternal exposure to smoking, alcoholism, poor nutrition, viral illness, medicines, and teratogens at the work place and at home in pregnancy are key contributors in aetiology, according to epidemiological and experimental research. Uncertainty exists regarding the impact of maternal nutrition, particularly multivitamins, in oro-facial clefts. Furthermore, in many of the poorest communities with both the highest percentages of oro-facial clefts, measurements of daily diet or biochemical measurements of nutritional intake are difficult to conduct and frequently unavailable. Socio-economic status is still a mystery, and more research is needed to understand the elements of deprivation and how they affect reproductive health. More precise exposure measurements and data pooling are required in future investigations.

Teratogen	Cleft type	Genetic Link
Alcohol	Cleft lip- cleft palate	MSX1, TGFb3
Cigarette Smoke	Cleft lip- cleft palate	TGFa
Folic acid	Cleft lip- cleft palate	TGFa, MTHFR
Steroids	Cleft lip- cleft palate	TGFb
Anticonvulsants	Cleft lip- cleft palate	GABA receptor
Altitude	Cleft lip	

Table 7. Environmental Causes of Orofacial Clefts

The main external conditions that have been linked to a greater risk of oro-facial cleft include alcohol intake, solvent use, tobacco use, and exposure to agricultural chemicals and solvents. There have also been reports that some anti-epileptic medication kinds raise the risk.

But it is a well-known fact that the chance of orofacial clefts recurring in siblings, as well as the risk that increases with the presence of two or more damaged siblings, is more than what can be expected by the family aggregation of environmental factors. Assessments of the comparative risk of a disease linked to an environmental factor can be greatly diluted if measures of genetic predisposition are not taken into consideration in epidemiological investigations. As a result, a potentially beneficial or teratogenic effect may be missed.

Tobacco and OFCs

With a community risk of up to 20%, maternal cigarette use during pregnancy has been repeatedly related to an elevated risk including both CLP and isolated CP. Passive smoking exposure has not been considered in most investigations, and in one recent case-control study in China that did consider maternal passive smoking, the odds ratio for CLP) was 1.8, suggesting that this relationship may be overestimated (95 percent CI, 1.2- 2.8). While smoking bans have been passed in some industrialised nations and tobacco sales have decreased, the New York Times of November 14, 2010, mentioned that large tobacco companies are stepping up their efforts worldwide to fight strict regulations on the marketing of cigarettes as sales to developing countries have become increasingly important.

Maternal Alcohol Use and OFCs

Fetal alcohol syndrome is well-known to be caused by maternal alcohol consumption; however, the impact of alcohol in solitary OFCs is less clear, with some research reporting beneficial connections while others did not. Alcohol use occurs in a wide range of social and dietary situations, some of which can have confounding or modifying impacts on diet, smoking, stress, or drug use. Negative results may not be widely publicised since publication bias is thought to be a problem for moderate alcohol use. There are numerous studies reporting on drinking alcohol while smoking than the other way around.

Maternal Metabolism, Nutrition, and OFCs

Although maternal diabetes, obesity, and other metabolic conditions have been linked to congenital abnormalities and have been reported to be connected with CL (P), these problems are still notably understudied in OFCs. Future OFC studies should focus on these issues because socioeconomic inequality has been connected to the pandemics of obesity and diabetes that have erupted in both rich and many developing nations. The discovery in a randomized clinical study that maternal peri-conceptional folic consumption reduces the frequency risk of neural tube defects has generated intense interest in the effects of nutritional status during in the peri-conceptional period on the event occurring of several congenital anomalies.

In both animal and human studies, the impact of maternal vitamin status during the preconception period has been disputed in relation to OFCs and other morphological birth defects like limb abnormalities, cono-truncal heart problems, and urinary tract malformations.

Vitamin Supplements

Even though assessments of food intake or biochemical markers of nutritional status are difficult to make and frequently unavailable in many of the most underprivileged communities with the greatest prevalence of OFCs, observational studies point to a function for maternal nutrition in OFCs. Future research should more precisely assess exposures, better manage confounding, and pool data. In a recent meta-analysis, mothers who used multivitamin supplements in the first trimester of pregnancy had a 25% lower birth prevalence of OFCs. A probable relationship between maternal hyperthermia while delivery and vitamin supplement use has been suggested by two studies, whereby supplementation reduces the elevated risk of CL (P) connected to hyperthermia.

Findings from various research make it difficult to tell which elements in multivitamins are beneficial as well as whether other healthy behaviours of multivitamin users skew the findings.

Folic Acid

It's unclear what part folic acid supplements or diet plays in human OFC. There is some indication of a decrease in the prevalence of CL at birth in North America, where it has required to fortify grain by folic since the late 1990s (P). Australia, where there is voluntary fortification, has not seen this. There was a decline in the US for all clefts combined, but not in Canada, Chile, or in the coupled data from the three South American nations. Case-control studies examining maternal food intake of folate, red cell and plasma folate, and multivitamin supplements containing folic acid had conflicting results. In a case-control research conducted in Utah, case moms' plasma and red blood cell folate levels were considerably lower than those of control mothers.

There weren't any differences in the usage of prenatal multivitamins, and the mean discrepancies in folate levels among cases and controls grew year after the damaged pregnancy; as a result, case moms may be more likely than control mothers to have a progressive abnormality of folate metabolism.

Other Specific Nutrients

There have been reports of higher mean maternal blood homocysteine levels in mothers of children with CL (P), which is somewhat correlated with folate status. In animal experiments, vitamin B-6 (pyridoxine and related substances) has been shown to decrease CL (P) and is a co-factor in the metabolism of homocysteine. In the Philippines and the Netherlands, biomarkers of low vitamin B-6 status were linked to an elevated risk of CLP. People that consume a lot of polished food in Asia are more likely to be vitamin B-6 deficient, and they also seem to have more CL (P). In animal research, zinc deficiency results in CP and other birth defects because zinc is essential for foetal development. In the Netherlands, mothers of kids with CL (P) had lower levels of erythrocyte zinc than control moms, and comparable variations were found in babies both with and without CLP. In the Philippines, where zinc deficiency is common, higher maternal blood zinc levels were linked, dose-dependently, to a lower incidence of CL (P). Zinc may be more of a concern for moms in undernourished nations, according to a study case of mothers in Utah that revealed no differences in plasma zinc levels. Riboflavin and vitamin A are additional substances that may contribute to the genesis of CLP. Although severe craniofacial deformities may develop in foetuses exposed to retinoid medicines, this finding may not be applicable to vitamin A intake from food sources.

Genetic-Environmental Interactions

The majority of the research on face clefting has looked at both genetic and environmental factors separately. There is complex interaction between the two, according to more recent research. Therefore, because of the combination of genetic vulnerability and exposure, certain population subgroups may have a considerably large or particularly low chance of developing clefts. Oro-facial clefts may be related to genetic variants associated with the metabolism of alcohol, chemicals in tobacco and smoke, as well as those engaged in nutritional metabolism. If pertinent data on these characteristics can be retroactively gathered from impacted families, hypotheses can be evaluated.

It is difficult to pinpoint the cause of non-syndromic clefts' aetiology in part because it is genetic factorial, with genetic disposition to environmental variables playing a significant role. Numerous studies have been conducted to look at potential connections that have been claimed to be tested because of the potential advantages to public health. These include the relationships between: TGFa (with smoking and vitamin supplements), TGFB3 (with smoking and alcohol), MSXI (with smoking and alcohol), polymorphisms influencing xenobiotic metabolism (e.g., genes coding for epoxy hydrolase, glutathione-S-transferase, and N-acetyl transferase) and smoking occupational exposures, maternal medication use, retinoic acid receptor alpha (RARA) polymorphism. Oro-facial clefting has been linked to maternal folic acid insufficiency. The maternal 5, 10-methylene tetrahydrofolate reductase enzymes may have a variation that reduces the enzyme's efficiency, which could account for this finding. More research indicates that the genotype of the mother may also affect the foetal folate status. It is becoming more obvious that minor interaction between both the environmental and genetic makeup make newborns prone to clefting as our knowledge of the etiology of cleft lip and cleft palate grows.

CHAPTER SIX

CLASSIFICATION

Classification schemes projected are on the basis of the morphology of cleft lip as well as cleft palate and few on the basis of values determined embryonically. Chief goal to recommend these particular schemes were to circumstance the preparation of subsequent management and treatment. Not limited to this, it also aids the patient in order to name, grade, recollect, strategise and converse about the clinical scenario. Few of these groupings include namely, "Tessier type, Veau, and Davis and Ritchie classifications."

"The American Cleft Palate Association" and "Kernahan and Stark classifications" happen to be recognised as the most preferred and recommended variable systems presently. The palate has constantly been incorporated into the classifications, occasionally with distinct description of clefts involving the hard palate, soft palate and also the uvula.

Cleft of the lip includes a diverse form of management. Few primary groupings legalised the surveillance of isolated occurring cleft defects of the lip, although many documented lip involving cleft defects merely as extensions of palatal clefts or overlooked these completely. The associated alveolar processes show an increased unpredictable contemplation. It is totally unattended in a few referred classifications or supplementary in the form of a step of fame along through its very particular citation. Sub mucous defect involves management ranging from wholesome exclusion to a distinct tentative mention.

'CLASSIFICATION BY DAVIS AND RITCHIE' (1922)

This particular grouping was recommended by 'Davis and Ritchie in 1922'. It was one of the very first classifications as mentioned in the literature. This classification system roughly categorized the cleft defects into three broad assemblies categorised on the basis of the position of cleft in approximation to the associated alveolar process.

"Group I- Pre alveolar clefts:

Unilateral cleft lip

Bilateral cleft lip

Median cleft lip

Group II - Post alveolar clefts:

Cleft hard palate alone

Cleft soft palate alone

Cleft soft palate and hard palate

Sub mucous cleft

Group III-Alveolar clefts:

Unilateral alveolar cleft

Bilateral alveolar cleft

Median alveolar cleft"

"CLASSIFICATION BY VEAU (1931)"

"Veau recommended the following grouping system in the year 1931

Group I (A) - Defects involving the soft palate only

Group II (B) - Defects involving the hard palate as well as soft palate extending not any further than that of the incisive foramen, thereby comprising of the secondary palate alone.

Group Ill (C) - Complete unilateral cleft, extending from that of the soft palate to the alveolus, commonly inclusive of the lip.

Group IV (D) - Complete bilateral clefts, more often resembles Group III but has a bilateral appearance.

When cleft is bilaterally present, pre-maxilla is observed to be suspended from the nasal septum."

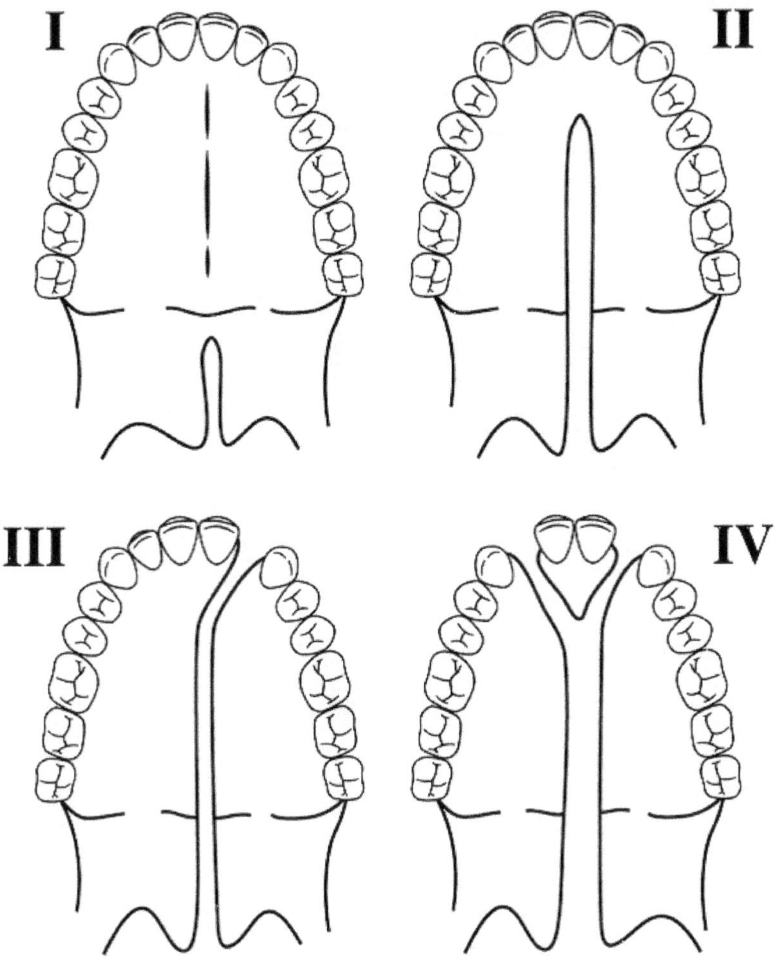

Figure 19: Diagrammatic presentation of Veau's classification

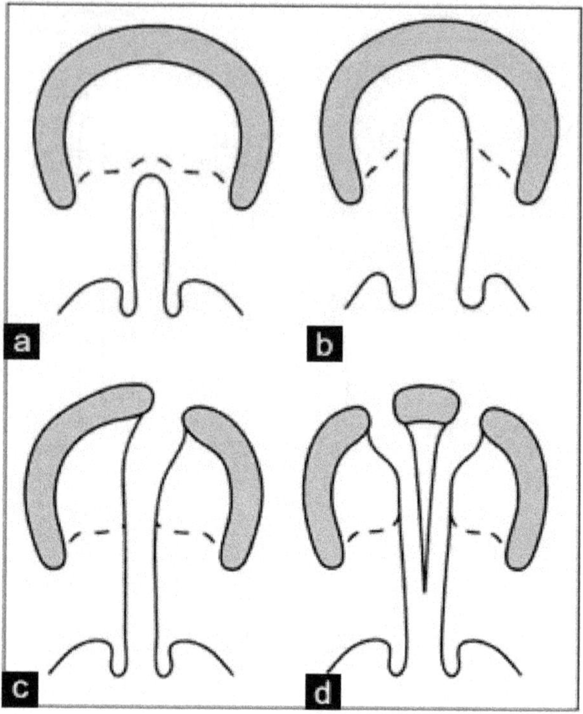

Figure 20: Diagrammatic presentation of Veau's classification

"CLASSIFICATION BY FOGH ANDERSON (1942)"

"Paul Fogh Anderson of Copenhegen defined and catergorized morphological system of grouping of cleft lip and cleft palate on the basis of embryological as well as genetical factors.

He allocated clefts involving defects among three catergorized:

Harelip existing a single or double, comprising all varied degrees acquired through a minor indentation in the pro-labium to a completely involving cleft defect of the lip outreaching "as far as the incisor foramen".

Harelip as well as cleft palate, which happens to be the major catergory. He illustrated completely involving cleft defects extending through the nostril involving the uvula. This particular group comprised of single as well as double clefts.

Cleft palate

- This particular category comprised of isolated occurring cleft defect of the palate which he illustrated that it might comprise of soft as well as hard part of palate along with the mostly median and it possibly never extends more than the associated incisor foramen. He happened to include sub mucous cleft defect showing presentation as a cleftal defect involving the soft part of palate existing only as a bony cleftal defect of hard part of palate with completely involving oral as well as nasal mucous membranes."

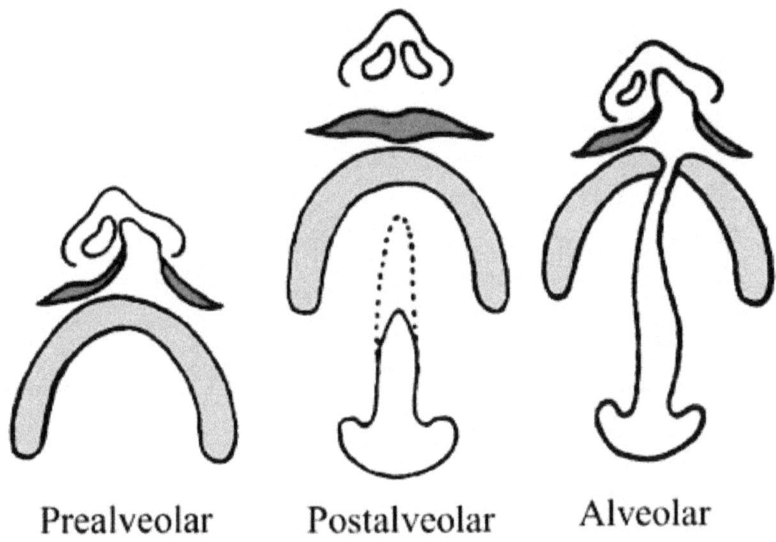

Figure 21: Diagrammatie presentation of Fogh Anderson's classification

"KERNAHAN AND STARK CLASSIFICATION (1958)"

"Kernahan and Stark recognized the need for a classification based on embryology rather than morphology. The primary palate denotes the lip, alveolar ridge and the pre-maxilla and the secondary palate refers to the hard and the soft palate which evolves from the maxillary shelves.

Clefts of primary palate only

Unilateral

- Complete
- Incomplete.

Median

- Complete (pre-maxilla absent)
- Incomplete (pre-maxilla rudimentary)

Bilateral

- Complete
- Incomplete

Clefts of secondary palate only

- Complete
- Incomplete, or Sub mucosal

Clefts of primary and secondary palate

- Unilateral (right or left)
- Complete or incomplete.

Median

-Complete or incomplete.

Bilateral

- Complete or incomplete."

SCHUCHARDT AND PFEIFER'S SYMBOLIC CLASSIFICATION

(1964)

"Schuchardt and Pfeifer's 99 was the first diagrammatic classification. It makes use of a chart made up of a vertical block of three pairs of rectangles with an inverted triangle at bottom. The inverted triangle represents the soft palate, while the rectangles represent the lip, alveolus and the hard palate as we go down. Areas affected by clefts are shaded on the chat. Partial clefts and total clefts were shaded in different colors. It is a relatively simple classification and ideal if printed graphs of the proposed chart were available. It was not easy to communicate as writing or typing was not possible."

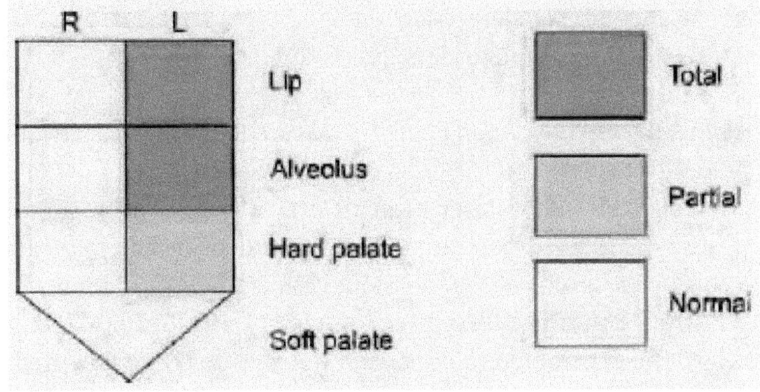

Figure 22: Diagrammatic presentation of Schuchardt and Pfeifer's classification

CLASSIFICATION BY ARTURO SANTIAGO (1969)

"Santiago A 100 proposed a classification in 1969 in which he used four digits to indicate presence of cleft and its location. Each digit is followed by letter to Indicate condition of cleft (complete, incomplete or sub mucous).

Four digits represent the following four structures affected by cleft

The first digit refers to the lip.

The second digit refers to the alveolus.

The third digit refers to the hard palate.

The fourth digit refers to the soft palate.

The numbers used as digits represents the condition of cleft.

0- No cleft

1 Midline cleft

2- Cleft on right side

3-Cleft on left side

4 Bilateral cleft

The letters indicate more specifically the type of cleft.

A -An incomplete midline cleft

B -An incomplete cleft of right side

C -An incomplete cleft of left side

D -Bilateral incomplete cleft

E- Sub mucous cleft

Points to consider when using the Arturo Santiago Classification System:

When a cleft is not described that it is complete or incomplete, it is always assumed as complete cleft. When clefts of lip, hard and soft palate are described without giving any information about alveolus, it is assumed that it is completely affected by cleft. All cases will be considered midline cleft unless otherwise specified."

KERNAHAN'S STRIPPED 'Y' CLASSIFICATION (1971)

"This is a symbolic classification given by Kernahan. The classification uses a stripped 'Y' having numbered blocks to represent a specific area of the oral cavity.

Block 1and 4 Lip

Block 2 and 5 - Alveolus

Block 3 and 6 - Hard palate anterior to the incisive foramen

Block 7 and 8 Hard palate posterior to incisive foramen

Block 9 Soft palate

The boxes are shaded in areas where the cleft has occurred."

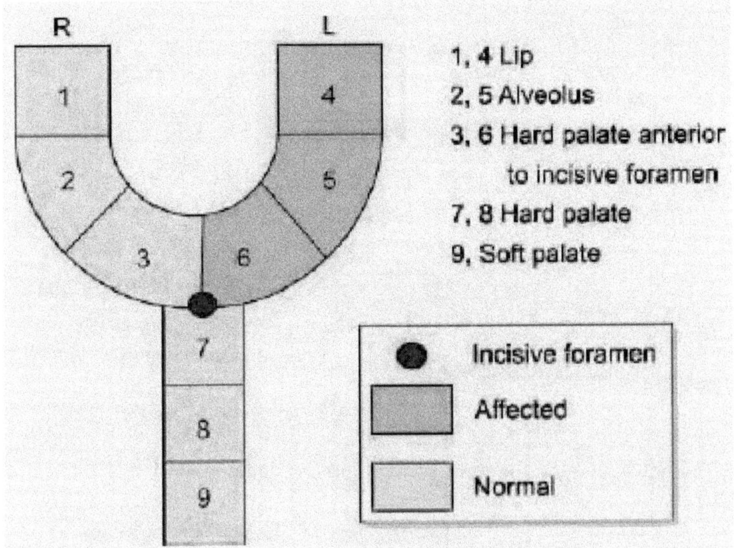

Figure 23: Diagrammatic presentation of Kernahan's Classification

"MILLARD'S MODIFICATION OF THE KERNAHAN'S STRIPPED "Y" CLASSIFICATION (1976)"

"Millard further supplemented two triangles over the tip of the "Y" to signify the nasal floor. This amplified the quantity of boxes to 11 as

Block 1 and 5- referring to the Nasal floor

Block 2 and 6- referring to the Lip

Block 3 and 7-referring to the Alveolus

Block 4 and 8-referring to the hard palate anterior to the incisive foramen

Block 9 and 10-referring to the hard palate posterior to the incisive foramen

Block 11- referring to the soft palate

The unaffected regions weren't shaded and the shading of the triangles signified the falsification of the nose."

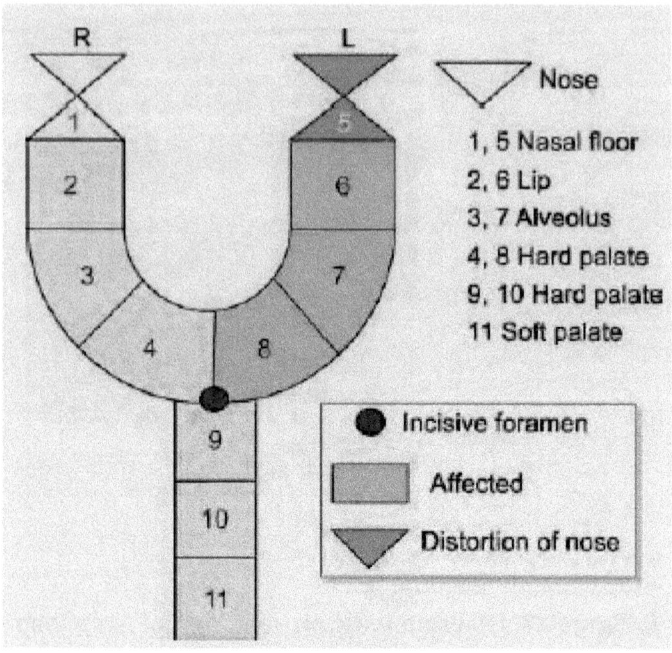

Figure 24: Diagrammatic presentation of millard's modification and Classification

"ELSAHY'S MODIFICATION OF THE KERNAHAN'S STRIPPED "Y" CLASSIFICATION (1973)"

"Elsahy 103 altered Stripped "Y" supplementary through double coating the associated blocks number 9 and 10 located in the region of the hard part of the palate as well as incorporated use of marked arrows in order to designate the involved course of deflection occurring in completely involving clefts. He similarly located a circle number 12 located underneath the stem portion of the "Y" in order to characterise part of pharynx as well as also a definite spotted streak running through the y to that of the part of circle numbered 12 imitating velo-pharyngeal proficiency. Additional circle 13 was likewise supplementary to characterise the pre-maxilla and also the quantity of its protuberance was designated with the help of scattered line."

"LAHSHAL CLASSIFICATION OF CLEFT LIP AND PALATE (1989)"

"Kriens 104 proposed LAHSHAL, an abbreviated documentation system in 1987. Lahshal is a paraphrase of the anatomic areas affected by the cleft.

L- Lip
A-Alveolus
H-Hard palate
S-Soft palate
H-Hard palate
A-Alveolus
L-Lip

This classification is based on the premise that clefts of lip, alveolus and hard palate can be bilateral while clefts involving the soft palate are usually unilateral. The areas involved in the cleft are denoted by the specific alphabet standing for it."

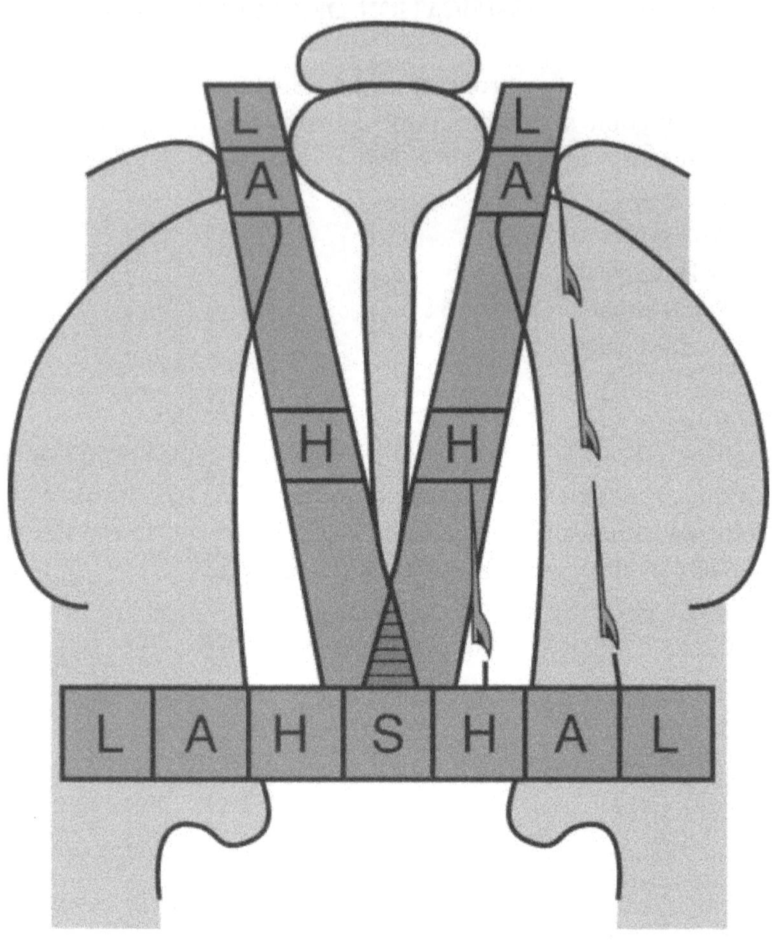

Figure 25: Diagrammatic presentation of LAHSHAL Classification

"INTERNATIONAL CONFEDERATION FOR PLASTIC AND RECONSTRUCTIVE SURGERY CLASSIFICATION (1968)"

"Group I: Clefts of Anterior (Primary) Palate

a. Lip: right and/or left

b. Alveolus: right and/or left.

Group II: Clefts of Anterior and Posterior

(Primary and secondary) palate:

a. Lip: right and/or left

b. Alveolus: right and/or left

c. Hard palate: right and/or left.

Group III: Clefts of Posterior (Secondary) Palate

a. Hard palate: right and/or left

b. Soft palate: medium.

For further subdivision the terms ’total‘ and ’partial‘ should be used.”

“RARE FACIAL CLEFTS CLASSIFICATION BASED ON TOPOGRAPHICAL FINDINGS”

“a. Median clefts of upper lip with or without hypoplasia or aplasia of pre-maxilla

b. Oblique clefts (oro-orbital)

c. Transverse clefts (oro-auricular)

d. Clefts of lower lip, nose, and other very rare clefts.

In the international classification, several problems are apparent.

Numbering of groups may cause confusion with the classification of Veau and Davis and Ritchie (1972). The term anterior palate is used rather than primary palate" (Kernahan and Stark, 1955) or pre-palate (ACPA) 1968.

Median clefts are enumerated under the category of facial clefts somewhat than clefts defect of the lip. Lip is not truly an embryologic part of the "primary palate.”

AMERICAN CLEFT PALATE ASSOCIATION (1962)

“1. Clefts of Pre-palate

Cleft lip

Unilateral - Right, left, extent in thirds

Bilateral - Right, left, extent in thirds

Median -Extent in thirds

Pro-labium -Small, medium, large

Congenital scar -Right, left, medium Extent in thirds

Clefts of the alveolar process
Unilateral - Right, left, extent in thirds
Bilateral- Right, left, extent in thirds
Median- Extent in thirds, sub mucous right, left, median
Cleft of pre-palate
Any combination of foregoing type
Pre-palate protrusion Pre-palate rotation
Pre-palate arrest (median cleft)
2. Clefts of Palate
Cleft of soft palate
Postero-anterior in thirds width (maximum in mm)
Palatal shortness - None, slight, moderate and marked
Sub mucous cleft - Extent in thirds
Cleft of the hard palate
Postero-anterior in thirds width (maximum in nm)
Vomer attachment - Right, left, absent
Sub mucous cleft- Extent in thirds"

CLASSIFICATION BY MORTIER'S

"Mortier et al (1997) developed a dual scale, which included two indicators. One corresponding to the severity of the cleft (ISS, or initial severity score) and another related to the surgical result (PRS, or postoperative results score). This indicator considered seven features to describe the patient. A comparison of the ISS and PRS allows for more objective judgement of the surgical result. However, it has been applied only to unilateral incomplete %.

Clefts of the primary palate, while these approaches attempt to characterize many features of primary and secondary palate clefts, a methodology still does not exist to adequately characterize other important features that relate to complete clefts, such as magnitude of segment separation. That is, the repair of a complete primary palate cleft with segment separation of 15 mm undoubtedly involves greater surgical complexity than one with segment separation of only 3 mm. None of the representational forms proposed to date for primary palate clefts considers this important parameter. In addition, elements associated with the patient's esthetics and functionality is considered only in a limited fashion. Therefore, a new approach to the description of primary and secondary cleft palates was proposed incorporating an element that are related to the palate, lip, and nose and that reflects their complexity from a surgical perspective. This work was developed jointly with the cleft lip and palate team at Pediatric Hospital of Tacubaya, which belongs to the Health Institute of the Federal

District Department in Mexico City, Mexico."

CLASSIFICATION BY ELNASSRY (2007)

"Elnassry proposed following classification in 2007. He divided cleft lip and palate patients in to seven classes.

Class I: Unilateral cleft lip

Class I1: Unilateral cleft lip and alveolus

Class II: Bilateral cleft lip and alveolus

Class IV: Unilateral complete cleft lip and palate

Class V: Bilateral complete cleft lip and palate

Class VI: Cleft hard palate

Class VII: Bifid uvula"

TESSIER'S CLASSIFICATION

"In 1976, Tessier proposed a classification system for facial clefts in which he described 14 different types of clefts according to their location in relation to eye and orbit. Tessier's classification system is commonly used by surgeons because it is purely descriptive and makes no pretence at causation and developmental relationships. There is also an ease of correlation between the anatomical defect and the required reconstructive surgery.

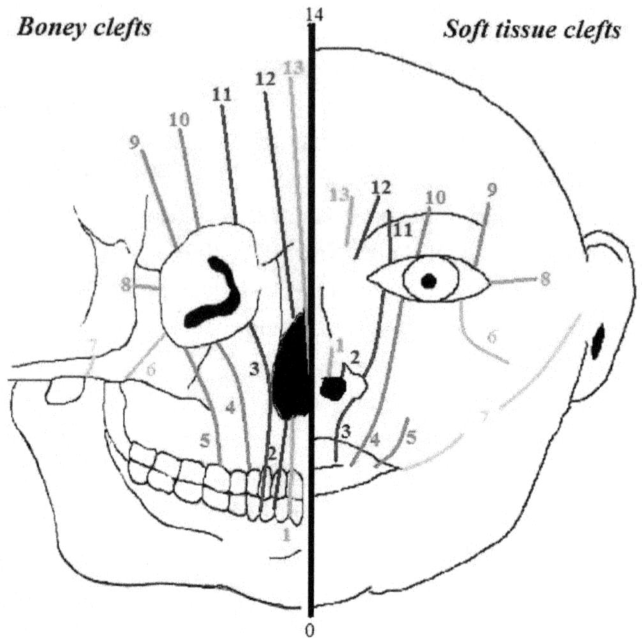

Figure 26: Diagrams of Tessier clefts; Soft tissue clefts of the face, number 0-14

Cleft is diagnosed when there is any interruption of either soft tissue (hair line, eyebrows, eyelids, nostrils, lips or ears) or skeleton. Clefts occur in well-defined places and along definite axes. They may be evaluated by their relationship in two main functional systems: the mouth and the eyes.

Bone and soft tissue are rarely involved to the same extent. From the midline to the infra orbital foramen, soft tissues defects are more frequent (or more destructive) than those of the skeleton. From the infra orbital foramen to the temporal bone, skeletal defects are more severe than soft tissue clefts, except for ear deformities.

Clefts occur in well-defined places. Description of clefts based on skeleton (rather than soft tissue) is easier because of the constancy of most skeletal points. Clefts are not seen along the course of a main vessel. Clefts in the skeleton do not imply absence of principal vessels or nerves in the area.

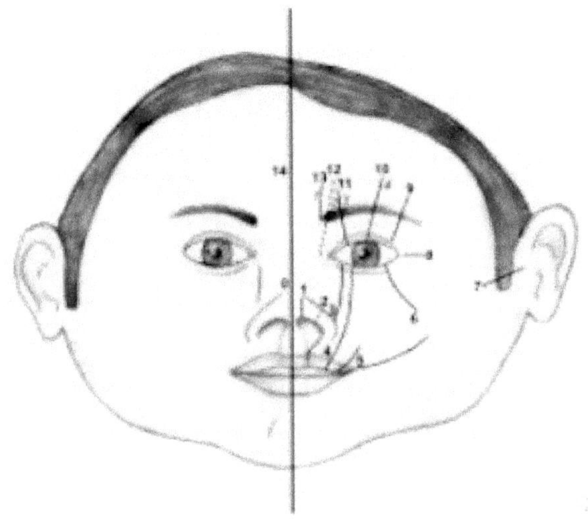

Figure 27: Diagrams of Tessier clefts; Bony clefts of the face, # 0-14

Clefts are situated along definite axes. Clefts of the upper lip, eyebrow, and frontal bone are often along the same axis as that of clefts of the cheek and lip. Clefts may be evaluated by their relationship with two main functional systems: either the lip and upper jaw, or the eyelids and orbital cavity. To orient, the orbit is described as two hemispheres: clefts running north through the upper lid are cranial; clefts running south through the lower lid are facial"

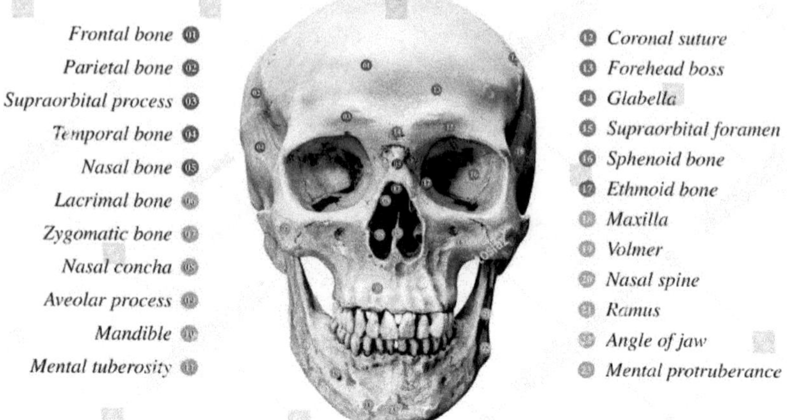

Figure 28: The bones of the face

CHAPTER SEVEN

TYPES OF OROFACIAL CLEFTS

"Depending upon the site, oro-facial cleft is divided into two parts

1. Cleft in facial Region
2. Cleft in oro-dental region

CLEFT IN FACIAL REGION

1. Cleft Lip
2. Oblique facial clefts
3. Lateral facial clefts
4. Median mandibular clefts

CLEFT IN ORO-DENTAL REGION

1. Cleft lip and cleft palate
2. Isolated cleft palate
3. Sub mucous cleft palate
4. Cleft of lip and alveolus
5. Cleft of the uvulae and soft palate
6. Cleft of uvulae alone

CLEFT IN FACIAL REGION

1. CLEFT LIP

Cleft of the lip is divided into 3 types:

A) Unilateral cleft lip -- Complete cleft lip/Incomplete cleft lip

B) Bilateral cleft lip -- complete cleft lip/incomplete cleft lip

C) Median cleft lip-- complete cleft lip/ incomplete cleft lip"

UNILATERAL AND BILATERAL CLEFT LIP

Cleftal defect of lip may be characterised as complete as and when extending through vermilion border upto recognised base of nose, else it might turned out to be recognised as an partial defect. There is presence of innumerous grades of partially involved cleft defects of the lip. Negligible defects concerning with vermilion border happened to be witnessed. For few cases, defect might encompass the part of nose being recognised as sub mucous cleft defect of the band of muscle, linked mainly by the help of the associated mucous membranes, skin as well as fibrous connective tissues. Depending on the length and breadth of the cleft defect, the nose alar cartilage on the affected side is arrested and deported and squeezed to a greater or lesser extent. The nose's tip, however, is diverging close to the side without a cleft deformity. The lip cleft may be unilateral or bilateral, occurring either on one or both sides, respectively. If it is bilateral, it may or may not equally constitute the lip on both ends depending on how it is proportional or asymmetrical. In the case of bilateral cleft abnormalities, it is crucial that the median region of a lip is isolated in the middle and has vestiges associated with the premaxilla and the columella. The identified portion of the philtrum is contained within this specific area of the lip. The pre-maxilla tends to dramatically advance the unique facial profile in full bilateral cleft lip abnormalities. Thus, it affects the nasal septum's section as well as the stalk-like vomer. Alar cartilages on either side of the columella appear to be trampled while a piece of it appears to be missing.

The effect on the affected facial profile emphasises the progression of the pre-maxillary position as well as the area of the lip that is affected to the surfaces of the face. The influence of the cleft defects on the alveolar processes increases with the severity of the lip deformity. Due to the ongoing relationship between the lip and the alveolar processes, it is unnecessary to include the alveolar processes as a separate unit in this specific description and classification. Even though the tegmen oris only contributes to the formation of the soft palate and the predominate section of the hard palate, the alveolar process of the maxilla rise from the mesoderm all around depths of the sulcus, unravelling the lip and the palate. It is interesting to note the correlation between the degree of the cleft's impact on the alveolar bone and deficiencies in both the permanent and deciduous dentition. The number of teeth, their specific shapes and structures, as well as their placement within the affected arch, can all be taken into consideration while evaluating the dental flaw.

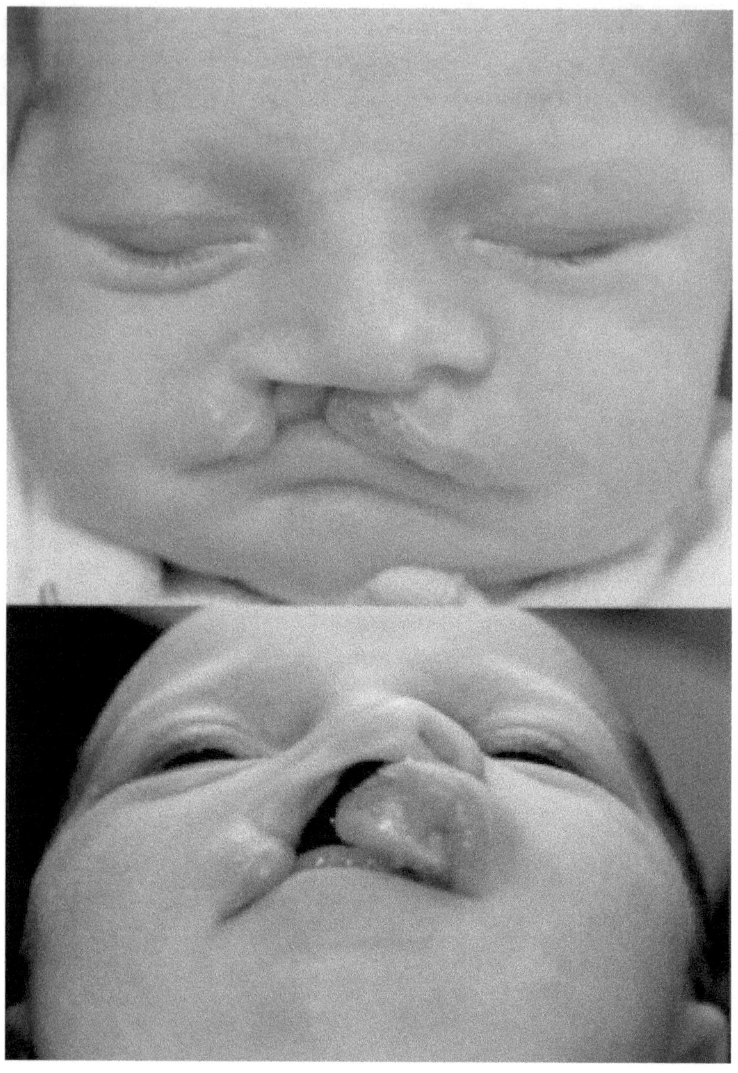

Figure 29: Complete unilateral cleft lip

In severe cases, the associated pre-maxillary section may be dislodged in the position of a non-cleft defect end of the tooth. Alveolar process abnormalities can range from tiny dimples in conjunction with limited cleft defects inside the lip to concretely discernible groove in a alveolar ridge. Minor grooves or dimples in the affected alveolar ridge have a propensity to close as the jaw grows. Though, the primary lateral incisor tooth that shows appearance in this particular region might be T shaped, or else distorted and also dislocated in the occlusal plane. Additional evidence regarding the emergence of teeth beside the cleft defects in the specific alveolar process should be provided by credentials of recognised papers and examination of serial records."

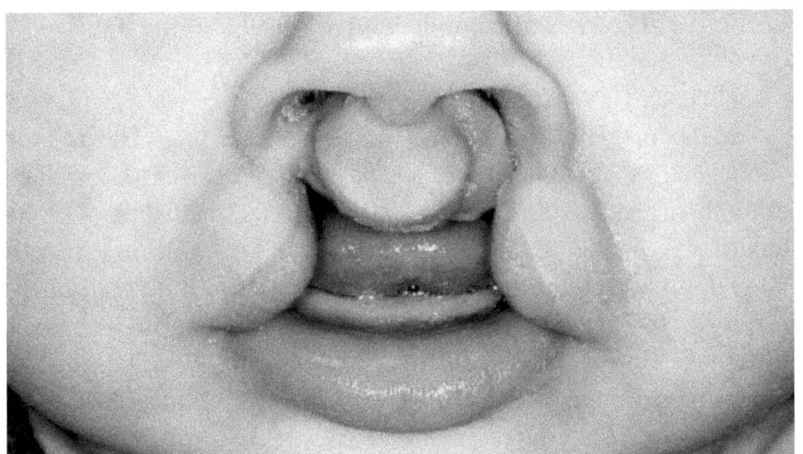

Figure 30: Complete bilateral cleft lip

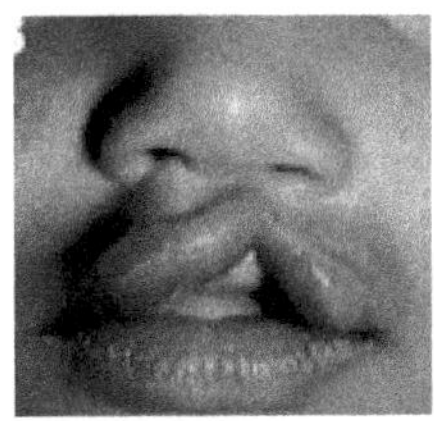

Figure 31: Incomplete unilateral cleft of the lip

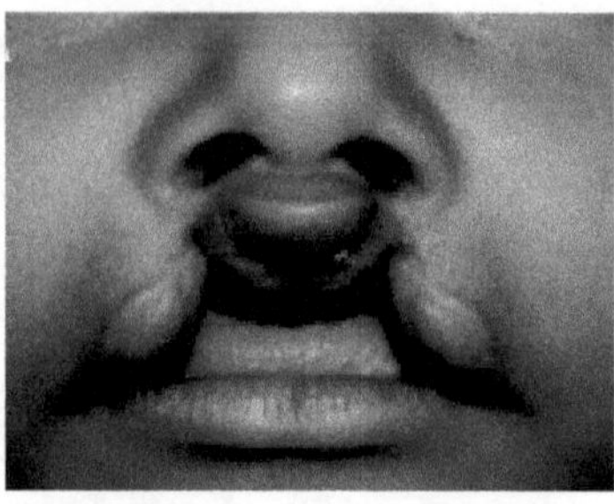

Figure 32: Incomplete bilateral cleft of the lip

MEDIAN CLEFT LIP

Median lip clefts are extremely uncommon, in contrast to cleftal abnormalities of the lateral lips. They are recognised in less than one out of every 100 cases of cleft palate and cleft lips, with an identifiable incidence range around 0.43 and 0.73 % for scenarios involving both conditions. Less than 0.0001 percent of all births result in the median development of cleft lips. Unfortunately, differences in race and gender have not been acknowledged. The failure of the 2 medial nasal processes involved to meet inside the centerline and then finally combine causes cleft lip abnormalities, a classifiable spectrum of deformity. However, the median lip cleft defect tends to heighten concerns about the super imposed face and brain that are not recognised in the commonly occurring lateral lip cleft deficits. The oro-facial-digital syndrome, which denotes a variety of anomalies of such face, head, hands, and feet, is one ailment that may be associated with an inadequately involved median cleft. Additional complete median cleft defects are seen to be of a syndromic presentation and existent as two distinct units, being the median cleft lip with hypoteloris as well as median cleft lip with hypertelorism. The circumference of the head falls between 2 known aberration of the mean and normotelorism when medial cleft lip deformity is present without holoprosencephaly.

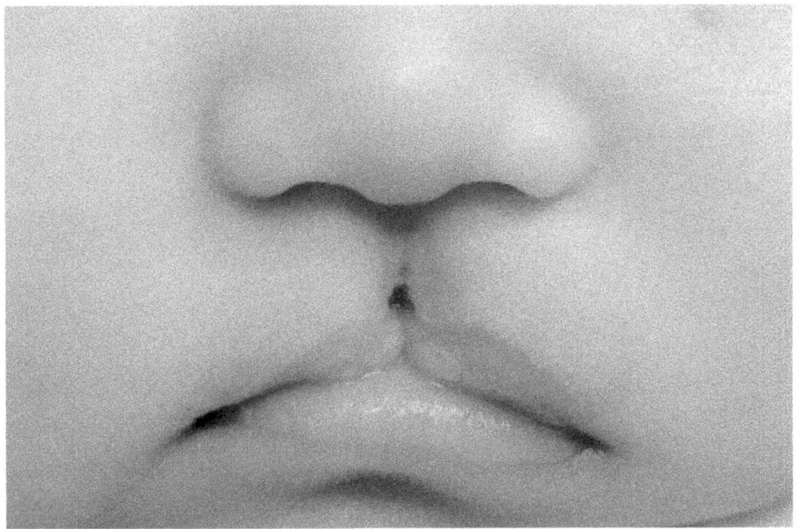

Figure 33: Incomplete median cleft lips. Vermilion notch, presence of central maxillary skeletal diastema, and double frenulum

As a result of inadequate anterior neural plate development and growth, holoprosencephaly results. The cerebrum becomes solitary compared to hemispheric in the absence of lateral evaginations in the typical holospheric telencephalon. The prosencephalic cavity so continues to be a monoventricle. The participation of embryologic cellular tissue, the prechordal mesoderm, in conjunction with roving neural crest cells, results in the concurrent median facial abnormalities. The fronto-nasal eminence of the prosencephalon gives further rise to the median craniofacial skeleton and also the cartilaginous septum. These specific embryonic tissues give rise to the super imposed soft tissues in a similar manner.

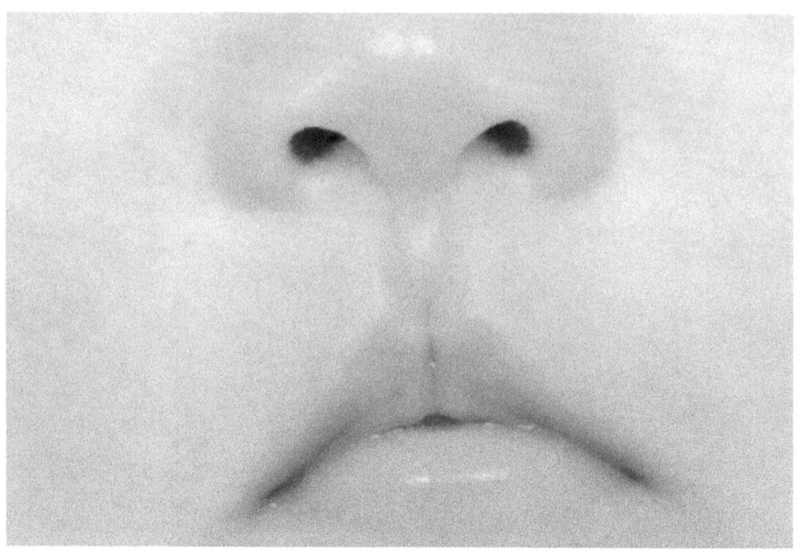

Figure 34: Incomplete median cleft lips. wider median cleft lip extending through the alveolus to the palate

The holoprosencephalic middle lip clefts are caused by developmental failure, in contrast to lateral lip cleft abnormalities, which show a problem with merging and subsequent fusing. The source, which are the brachial arches, clearly define the lateral precise properties of the concerned face, and as a result, they are typical. Even though the holoprosencephaly facial features are different and similar to those of brain development. The median cleft lip defect with hypotelorism happens to be categorised by absenteeism of the distinct crista galli, nasal as well as pre-maxillary bones and also nasal septum. The ethmoids characterised as hyperplastic complement not being the reason of the orbital hypotelorism, since it is chiefly existing as a brain defect. It is crucial to note that there are additional median cleft lip defects that develop and appear in a manner that is similar to holoprosencephaly but without cerebral involvement, as well as those that have varying degrees of distinguishing vomero-septal-prolabial hypoplasia. An intact ethmoid, nasal bone, and crista galli appear to be the most important and prominent structural changes in these affected people as related to conventional and traditional holoprosencephaly.

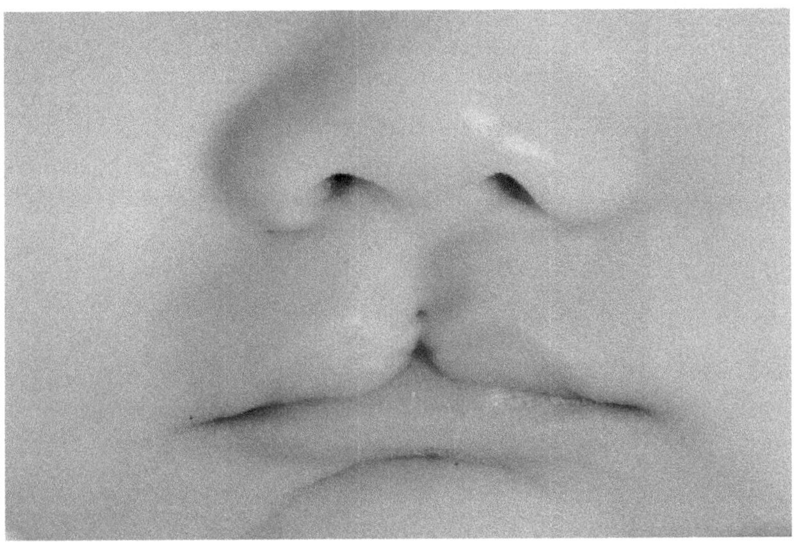

Figure 35: Median cleft lip in orofacial-digital syndrome

Recently, Muliken et al. identified a group of "syndromic"-appearing subjects who had typically been assigned a location on the "normal" end of the holoprosencephaly spectrum. The naso-maxillary hypoplasia, orbital hypertelorism, and concurrent unilateral and bilateral cleft lip-cleft palate defects are what distinguish these particular people.

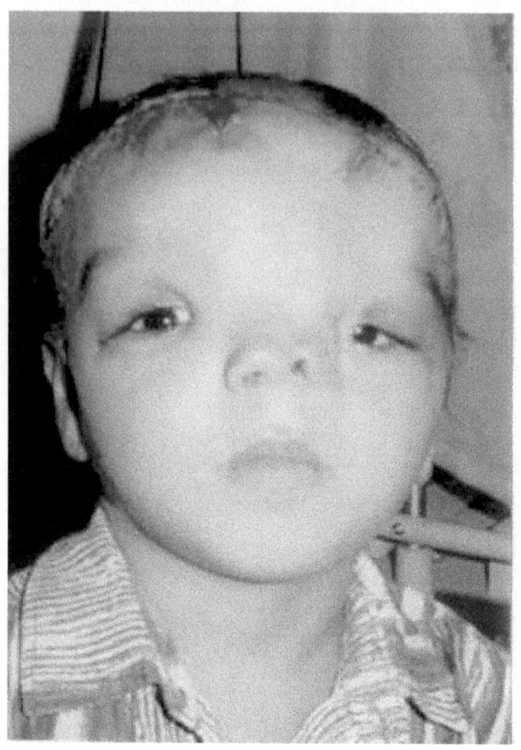

Figure 36: Holoprosencephalic facies with median cleft lip.

The frontonasal dysplasia, also known as median cleft face syndrome, is determined to be the outcome of the implicated facial processes' incomplete midline assimilation and varying degrees of lateralization. While the forebrain's morphogenesis is rarely complicated, its growth and development as a result is typically regular. The central cleft lip and palate deformity, bifid nose, hypertelorism of an eye, V-shaped frontal hairline becoming inferiorly displaced, and prominent cranium bifidum occultum are all features of fronto-nasal dysplasia, which is remarkably different from holoprosencephaly. Contrasting to occurring holoprosencephaly, the premaxillary segmen happens to be frequently existing while it is associated with a cleft defect and hence maxillary incisor outbreak can possibly be predictable.

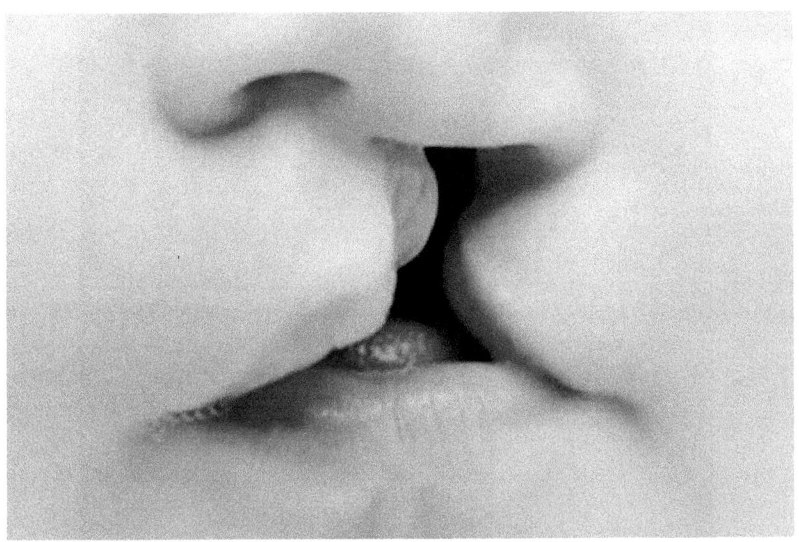

Figure 37: Vermilion notch, presence of central maxillary skeletal diastema, and double frenulum

Mutations of varius involved genes have seen to be associated and linked to the occurrence of holoprosencephaly. Though nonspecific and discrete craniofacial malformations comprising of median cleft lip defect have been seen to be established by plentiful supplementary mediators in the species of animals.

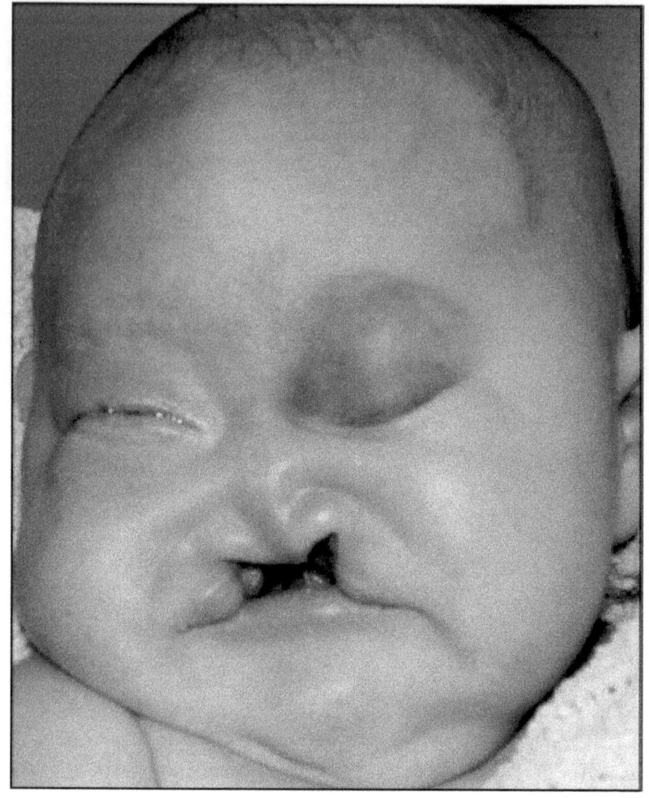

Figure 38: Holoprosencephalic facies with median cleft lip.

The clear teratogenic bases for why median problems develop in human species remain unaddressed. In rare cases, it has been observed that alcohol, specifically foetal alcohol syndrome, is associated with midline developmental flaws, including malformations of the median facial cleft.

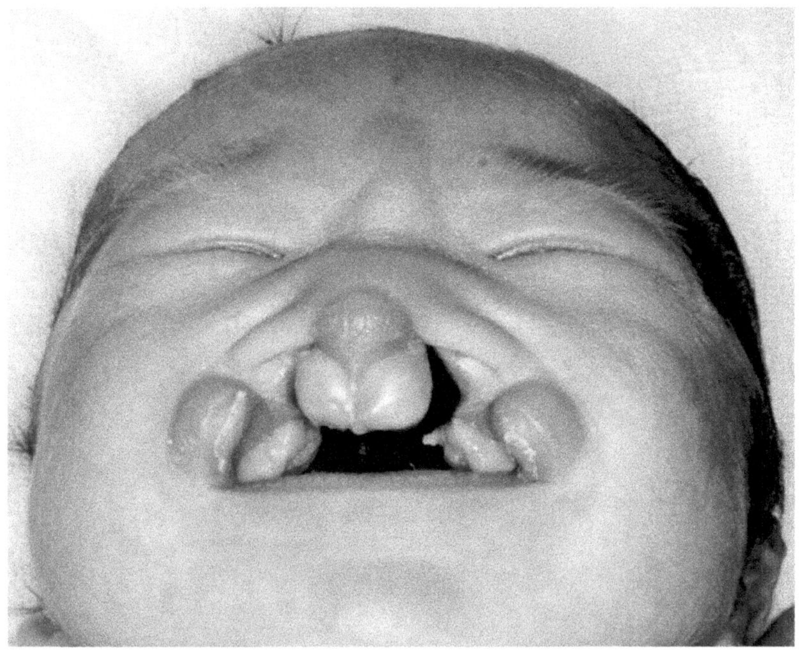

Figure 39: Vomero-septal-prolabial hypoplasia can be confuse with holoprosencephaly, but there is no upper craniofacial involvement

2. OBLIQUELY OCCURING FACIAL CLEFT

"The first report of an oblique facial cleft was made in 1732 by von kulmus and it is not surprising that he recorded it in Latin then in 1828 Delpech presented such case in French and in 1832 Walter dick of Glasgow reported one in English William rose of London in 1891 acknowledged his teacher Sir William Fergusson as the only English surgeon as far as he knew who had observed the rare facial cleft.

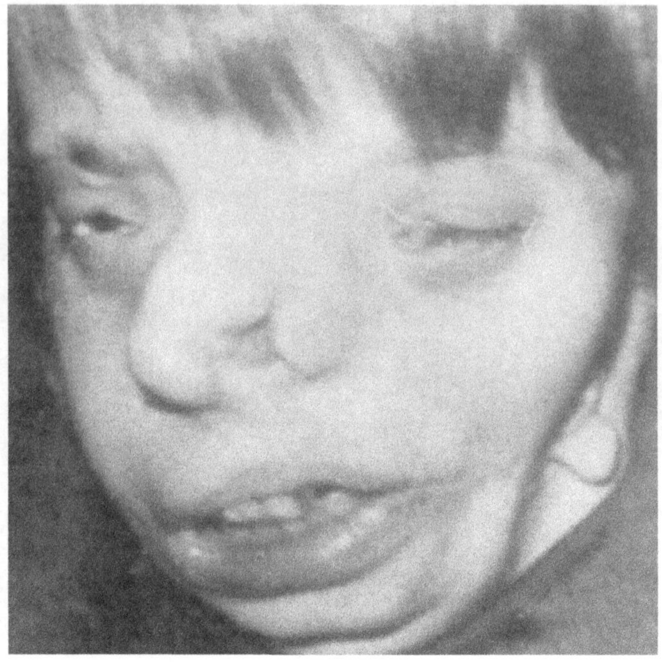

Figure 40: Differing degrees of expression of the median cleft face syndrome

The term oblique facial cleft, occurring in a variety of manifestations from the lip to the orbit, is a vague designation. The cleft has also been described by other equally nondescript names, including meloschisis and vertical facial and orbito-facial clefting.

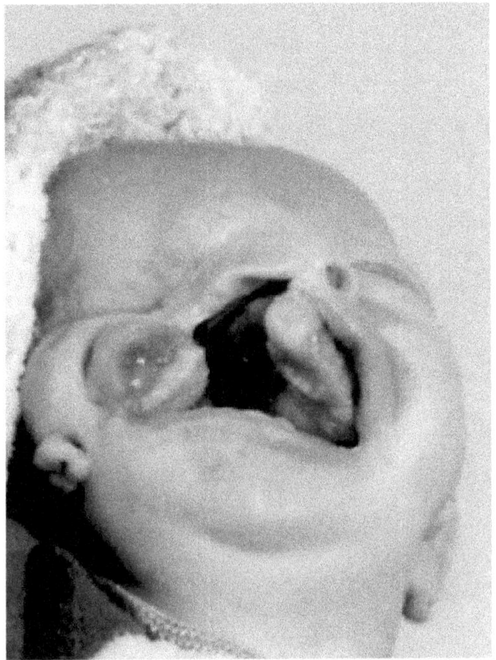

Figure 41: (Left) Incomplete median lip cleft with moderate widening of theinterorbital distance and nose.

It really represents a group of lateral mid-facial dysplasia's that consist of distinct malformations involving differing points of origin from the lip and superior extensions into the orbit. These clefts correspond to the Tessier cleft nos. 3, 4, and 5.

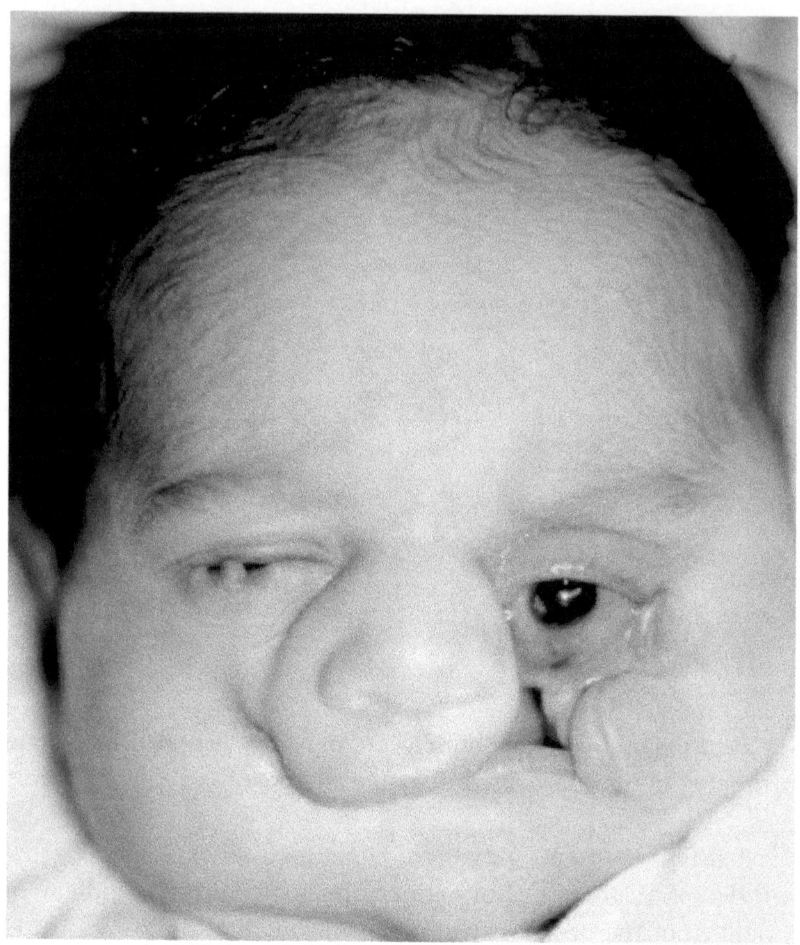

Figure 42: Tessier no. 4 orofacial cleft

The use of this nomenclature is of particular help in this area. Because of their rarity (less than 0.25 percent among all facial clefts) and incomplete case descriptions in the literature, the actual incidence of these clefts as a group and individually is not known. All known cases are sporadic, with no syndromic association or sex predilection.

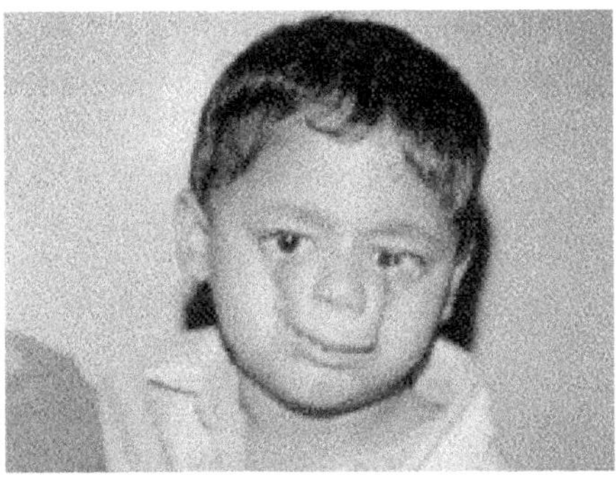

Figure 43: Bilateral incomplete Tessier no. 5 clefts

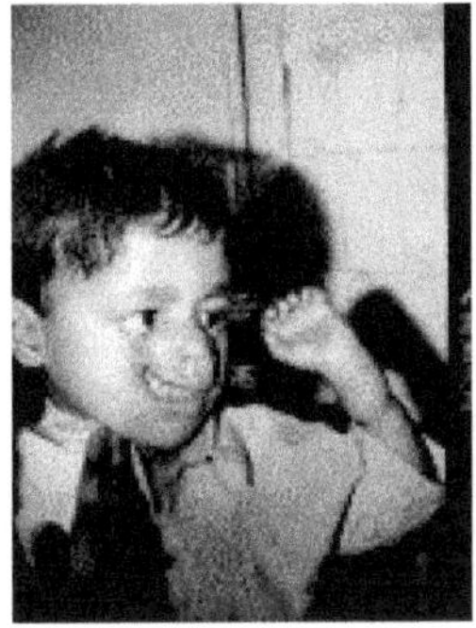

Figure 44: Bilateral incomplete Tessier no. 5 clefts

The oblique clefts, as indicated by Tessier cleft nos. 3 through 5, occur in slightly different regions of the lateral mid-face (cleft nos. 1 and 2 are best described as paramedian or vertical facial clefts and are excluded from this discussion). The most medial variety (cleft no. 3, also known as a naso-ocular or naso-maxillary cleft) extends from the philtrum of the lip, as occurs in the more common lateral cleft of the lip, to the medial canthus of the eye, with foreshortening of this distance. As a result, a bony cleft occurs at the lateral incisor/canine area of the alveolus, extending through the frontal process of the maxilla to the lacrimal groove of the medial orbit. Soft tissue defects, including colobomas of the nasal ala and lower eyelid and an inferiorly displaced medial canthus and globe, are characteristic.

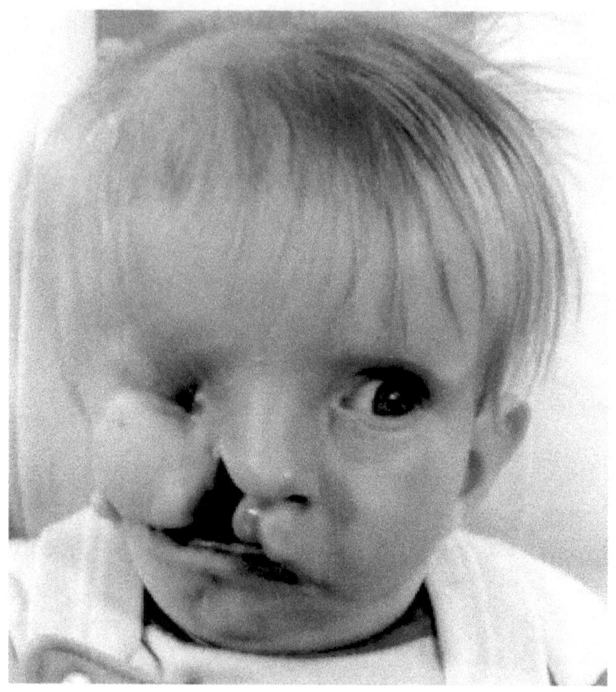

Figure 45: Holoprosencephalic facies with median cleft lip.

Concurrent absence or dysfunction of the nasolacrimal system is predictably high. More laterally, the cleft no. 4 (also known as an oro-ocular cleft) spares the nose and extends toward a more centric orbital position. The lip origin of this cleft deviates from common lip clefts and does not violate the philtral ridge. At a point between the philtrum and commissure, the cleft extends superiorly through the naso-labial fold and passes into the orbit just medial to the infra-orbital foramen (Fig. 23). As such, the medial canthal tendon and nasolacrimal duct are usually intact. However, a marked coloboma of the lower eyelid is present, and in some cases, varying degrees of anophthalmos are present.

The no. 5 cleft is primarily distinguished from the more medially positioned cleft no. 4 by passing lateral to the infra-orbital foramen (Fig. 24). This skeletal pathway difference has long been recognized and has historically (pre-Tessier) been subdivided into type I (no. 4) and type II (no. 5) forms of oro-ocular clefting" This specific cleft defect's lateral involvement contrasts sharply just at alveolar level by initiating posterior to that of canine. Additionally, it is believed that the symptoms pertaining to the eyes, which include an unmodified lower eyelid coloboma, inferior displacement, partial protrusion of the orbital contents into the sinus, and anophthalmos, are discordant findings that are occuring in a number 4 established cleft defect. Advanced and novel untried effort proposes that these particular abnormalities are reasoned to occur due to a amalgamation of unswervingly fastened migration of tissue and amplified local pressure that happens to establish distinct cellular ischemia. Consequently, cleft defects may seem to be established advanced in the stages of fetal growth and development other than throughout primary facial process of morphogenesis.

According to the committee of nomenclature belonging to the American Association distinct for rehabilitation and restoration of cleft palate defect there are two chief arrangements of obliquely involving facial cleft defects, the naso-ocular and also the oro-ocular defects. The relationship between the cleft as well as the infra orbit foramen further divides the oro-ocular type among medial and lateral groups."

NASO-OCULAR CLEFT

"Naso-ocular clefts are considered the result of failure of mesoderm migration or merging to obliterate the embryonic grooves between the naso-medial naso-lateral and maxillary prominences with each other. The naso-ocular cleft extends from the pyriform aperture to the medial canthal area along the approximate course of the nasolacrimal duct as the nasolacrimal duct is intact only in the mild cases it is usually absent or opened."

ORO-OCULAR CLEFT

"In oro-ocular clefts the fissure extends from the mouth to either the medial or the lateral canthus leaving the pyriform aperture intact the subgroup medial or lateral of the oro-ocular cleft s determined by the clefts position in relation to the infra orbital foramen. These clefts can occur in complete and incomplete forms, mild incomplete

Oro-ocular clefts can be confused with mild incomplete lip clefts and can be distinguished from them by two main characteristics.

1. The cleft lies lateral to the peak of the cupids bow rather than through it as in the standard cleft

2. Because of shortening of the soft tissue element on the affected side there is an upward tilt of the alar base instead of the usual downward flare

The oro-ocular type is subdivided into medial and lateral depending on the relationship of the cleft to the infra orbital foramen."

THE MEDIAL ORO-OCULAR CLEFT

"Medial oro-ocular clefts are considered the result of failure of mesoderm migration or merging to obliterate the embryonic grooves between the naso-lateral or naso-medial prominences and the maxillary prominences. The naso-medial and naso-lateral prominences having merged with each other successfully the cleft lies medial to the infra orbital foramen and instead of involving the nose bypasses it running upward in the region of the naso-labial cheek groove to terminate in the inner canthus of the lower eyelid. This fissure may extend up into the forehead usually in the temporal region and when the bone is cleft the split lies between the lateral incisor and the canine although the nose is well formed in unilateral cases it is usually rotated around its long axis in bilateral cases the bony and cartilaginous nose is detached from its lateral bony segments drawn upward with forward protrusion the orbit is sometimes shifted downward and is capacious because of the irregular and deficient growth of its walls"

THE LATERAL ORO-OCULAR CLEFT

"Lateral oro-ocular clefts do not correspond to any embryonic grooving. The lateral oro-ocular cleft extends from the angle of the mouth upward to the orbit terminating in the lateral canthus or in coloboma in the mid-portion of the lower lid lateral to the infra orbital foramen more often than in the naso-ocular type, incomplete forms occur in which the central portion of the cleft in the region of the cheek is replaced by scar like groove in mild cases. The nasolacrimal duct is intact but in severe cases it is defective or absent this is mysterious cleft it has the same origin as transverse cleft but its direction turns oblique not corresponding to any of the known embryonic facial grooves karfik in 1969 called it the true oblique cleft."

3. LATERAL FACIAL CLEFTS

"Lateral facial clefts, or commissural clefts, are best thought of as a variable finding within the broader congenital condition of hemi-facial microsomia (Tessier cleft no. 7).They are the second most common oro-facial cleft (second to the common cleft lip), with an incidence less than that of hemi-facial microsomia (one in 3500 to 5000 live births) because of an inconsistent occurrence within the syndrome. Although commissure clefts are not seen in every case of hemi facial microsomia, their occurrence should initiate a search for involvement of the ipsilateral ear, mandible, and facial nerve and overlying facial soft-tissue deficiencies. These clefts also occur in the oculoauriculovertebral spectrum (historically referred to as Goldenhar syndrome), which has the additional features of epibulbar dermoids, vertebral anomalies, and central nervous system and cardiopulmonary defects

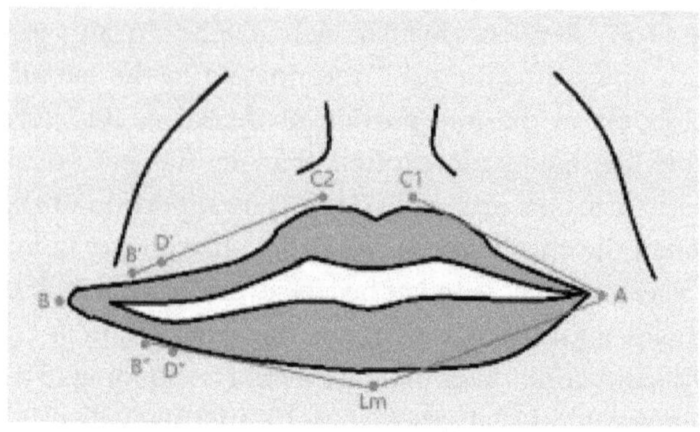

Figure 46: Tessier no. 7 (commissure) clefts.

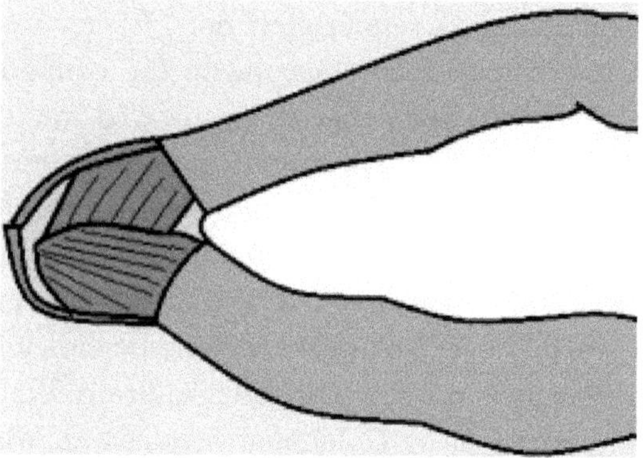

Figure 47: Tessier no. 7 (commissure) clefts.

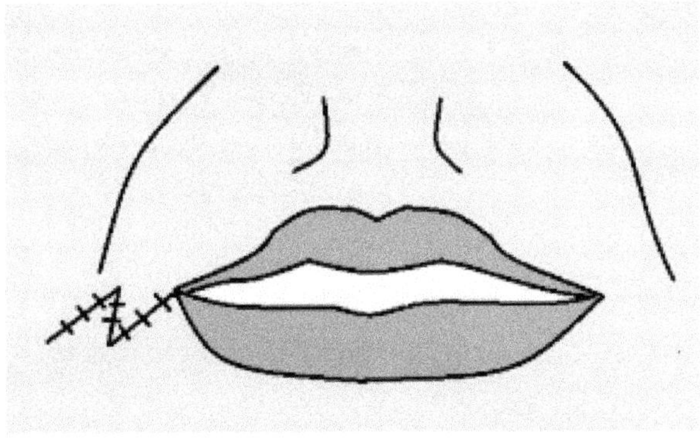

Figure 48: Tessier no. 7 (commissure) clefts.

The clinical findings of the lateral oral cleft variably extend along a line from the commissure to the tragus. Most commonly, a 1- to 3-cm-long cleft is present, with disruption of the orbicularis and buccinator muscles and with the cleft edges lined by vermilion. Only rarely does a complete cleft extend posterior to or beyond the anterior border of the masseter muscle, although a groove or skin depression continuing along the cleft line to the ear may occasionally be seen (Fig. 25). Because of the association between lateral oral clefts and hemi facial microsomia, underlying deformities of the mandible are well appreciated Less appreciated but equally common, particularly in severe expressions of the syndrome, is the zygomatico-orbital dysplasia, marked by a disruption of the zygomatic arch and inferior displacement of the lateral canthus caused by variable amounts of accompanying zygomatic hypoplasia and resultant orbital dystopia.

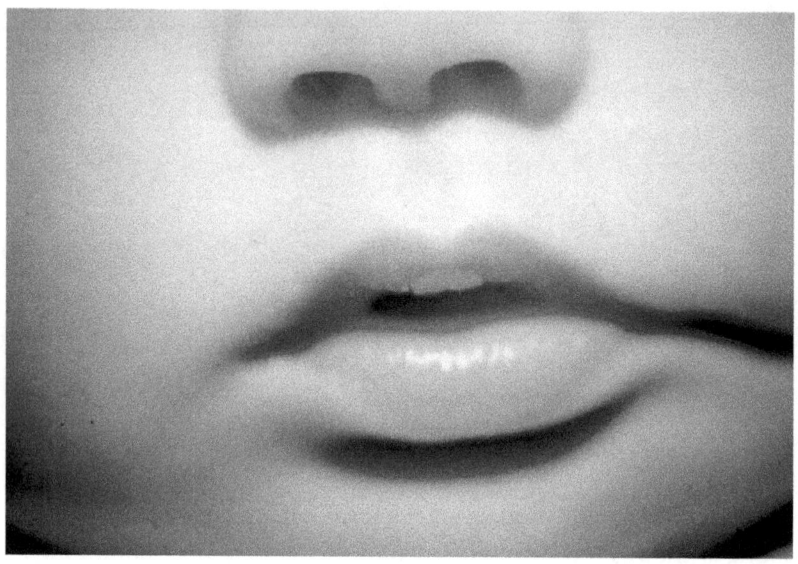

Figure 49: Tessier no. 7 (commissure) clefts. (Below, left) Rightsided hemifacial microsomia with commissural cleft extending to the anterior border of the masseter.

Lateral facial clefts are easy to understand embryologically, as the commissure represents the most anterior point of mesodermal merging of the maxillary and mandibular processes. Should the fusion process remain incomplete, a variable spectrum from furrowing of the tissues to complete anatomical separation persists.

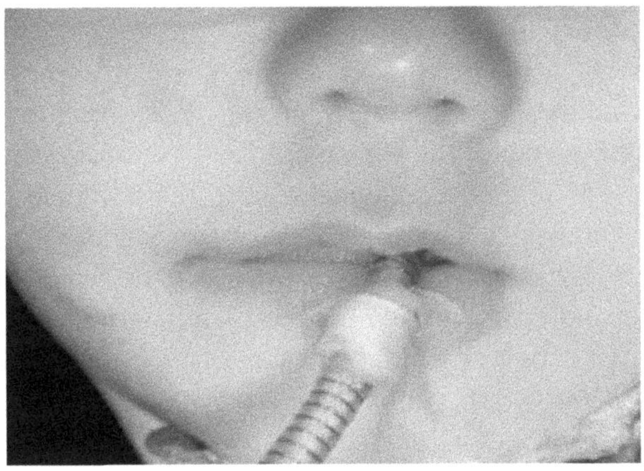

Figure 50: Tessier no. 7 (commissure) clefts. (Right) Bilateral commissural clefts without hemifacial microsomia

The pathogenesis of the lateral facial cleft appears to be heterogeneous. A vascular cause, attributable to embryonic hematoma formation from disruption of the stapedial artery stem, is one proposed mechanism. The severity of the condition subsequently depends on the size of the hematoma and its time course of resolution as brachial arch development occurs. The cause of this embryonic hemorrhage has been speculated to range from vascular flow anomalies, such as hypertension and hypoxia, to pharmacologic agents, such as salicylates and anticonvulsants. Intrauterine compression secondary to oligohydramnios in the embryonic head region has also been suggested and may account for some cases of hemi facial microsomia that occur with other anomalies, such as limb reduction defects."

4. MEDIAN MANDIBULAR CLEFTS

"Clefting of the lower face (Tessier cleft no. 30) almost universally occurs through the midline of the lip and mandible. Although paramedian lower lip/mandibular clefting has been reported, there are fewer than reported cases in the literature, appearing with less frequency than the oblique facial clefts. Sex and racial predilections remain indeterminate. A range of inferior clefting has been reported that extends from mild notching of the lower lip and mandibular alveolus (Fig 26) to complete cleavage of the mandible, extending into inferior neck structures. Tongue involvement is typical though variable in expression, ranging from a bifid anterior tip with ankyloglossia to the bony cleft margins, to marked lingual hypoplasia. Inferior cervical defects (midline separation, hypoplasia, and agenesis) of the epiglottis, strap muscles, hyoid bone, thyroid cartilage, and sternum may also be present, particularly when the cutaneous cleft passes caudal to the gnathion point on the chin. The embryologic basis of median mandibular clefts lies in the failure of coaptation of the free ends of the first visceral arches in the midline.

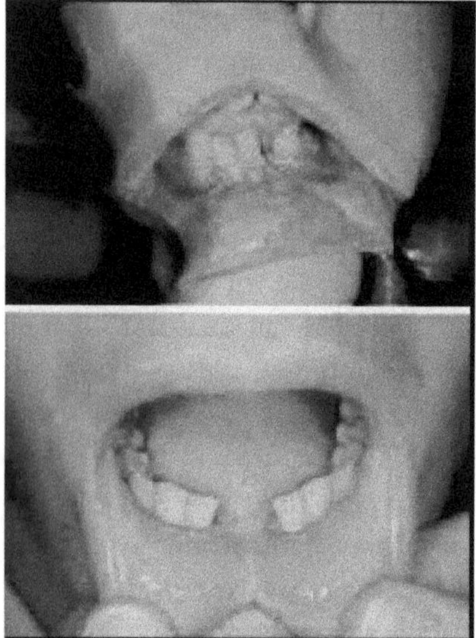

Figure 51: Median mandibular clefts. (Above) Vermilion notch of lower lip with central incisor diastema; (below) median cleft defect

extending through the lower lip and alveolus with ankyloglossia

Once the arches are formed through neural crest cell migration, vascularization, and mesodermal myoblastic ingrowth, growth centers are organized at their tips that are responsible for closing the final gap and coalescing the two sides. As the incisor teeth are frequently missing along the medial mandibular margins, this suggests that partial or complete failure of growth center differentiation and development is responsible for such defects rather than a simple merging and contact maintenance. Because no animal models exist for study of the median cleft lip, the cellular basis for this defect may remain unknown for some time. Presumably, however, more inferior cervical defects would be caused by similar mechanisms in the second and third visceral arches. The occasional association of a superior midline defect (cleft palate) with a median mandibular cleft is interesting because it suggests that a broader defect in epithelial mesenchymal merging and fusion is occurring or that the tongue abnormality affects palatal shelf closure in utero in these patients."

CLEFT IN ORO-DENTAL REGION

1. CLEFT LIP AND CLEFT PALATE

"Clefts of both the lip and palate may be unilateral or bilateral. They may be complete or incomplete. In a complete unilateral cleft of the lip and palate, a direct communication exists between the oral and nasal cavities on the side of the palate where the cleft is situated. The nasal septum is attached to the palatal process on the opposite side, thus separating the nasal chamber from the oral cavity.

A remarkable range of variation exists in each category. Indeed, various degrees of incompleteness of the cleft in the lip and palate may exist in combinations too numerous to describe conveniently. Moreover, some unilateral clefts of lip and palate exhibit wide separation of the palatal shelves. Others exhibit less separation, and in some cases, the segments actually overlap. The palatal segment on the side of the cleft is often tilted medially and upward. The vomer is deviated from the midline at the line of attachment to the palatal process on the non-cleft side. This deviation may be so extreme that the vomer assumes a nearly horizontal position at its inferior margin. The bilateral cleft lip and palate also may be complete or incomplete. If incomplete, it may be symmetrical or asymmetrical, depending on the equality of involvement on both sides. In the complete bilateral cleft 11p and palate, both nasal chambers are in direct communication with the oral cavity. The palatal processes are divided into two equal parts, and the turbinates are clearly visible within both nasal cavities. The nasal septum forms a midline structure that is timely attached to the base of the skull, but is fairly mobile in front where it supports the pre-maxilla and the columella.

Cephalometric roentgenograms reveal the existence of a suture line, the pre-maxillary vomerine suture, between the vomer and the pre-maxilla. This suture plays an important role in facial growth, and is also a point of flexion for the pre-maxilla upon the vomer. The pre-maxilla may be small or large, symmetrical or asymmetrical. The number of incisor teeth contained in this segment is directly related to its size and shape. Permanent teeth may be missing and it may contain only one or more deciduous teeth when the cleft of the lip is complete on both sides, the pre-maxilla projects considerably forward from the facial aspect of the maxillae. This anterior protrusion is less evident if the lip is incompletely cleft on one or both sides."

2. ISOLATED CLEFT PALATE

"In this defect, neither the lip nor the alveolar process is involved. The cleft may involve only the soft palate or both the soft and hard palates, but never the hard palate alone. This observation is in accordance with the finding that fusion of the hard and soft palates proceeds from front to back. The cleft may extend forward from the uvula to varying degrees. In some cases, the cleft is limited to the uvula or to the uvula and soft palate. In others, it may extend into the hard palate. It is recommended that a digital examination of the posterior edge of the hard palate be performed. A midline notching will reveal the presence of a sub mucous cleft. The full extent of sub mucous clefts can be mapped by cephalometric laminagraphy or by transillumination through the nose. In the extreme form, the cleft palate may extend anteriorly as far as the naso-palatine foramen, the incisal canal. When the cleft involves a considerable portion of the hard palate, the nasal chambers are in direct communication with the oral cavity. In most instances, the nasal septum is not attached to either palatal process throughout the extent of the cleft. However, occasional asymmetries may be noted in which the septum 15 attached to a portion of the palatal process on one side to a greater extent than to the palatal process on the opposite side. The outline of the cleft may be wide or narrow, pyriform or V-shaped. Excessively wide dental arches often are associated with wide clefts that extend to a considerable degree into the hard palate. In such instances, the mandibular dental arch may be in complete lingual relation to the maxillary arch so that the cusps of the teeth do not inter digitate in occlusion.

Lateral cephalometric head plates reveal that the dorsum of the tongue, at rest, is elevated and postured within the nasal cavity. During deglutition the thrusting action of the tongue operates to separate the palatal processes. These abnormalities in the posture and movements of the tongue are supported by the observations of speech pathologists. In this type of cleft, the vomer is significantly different in size and form from that observed in bilateral cleft lip and palate. In both types, the vomer is seen as a midline structure extending downward from the base of the skull. However, in bilateral cleft lip and palate, the inferior border of the vomer is thick and rounded, whereas in this category - cleft palate only - the vomer is thin and knife-edged. Serial observations reveal that the pattern of growth exhibited by the vomer is different in these two types of clefts. Several other distinguishing characteristics apparent in some of the clefts in this category merit further comment.

The high incidence of mandibular micrognathia found in patients with cleft palate gives credence to the theory that during embryonic development the tongue did not sink below the palatal processes, and thereby prevented their fusion in the midline. This raises the question of whether more than one causal mechanism might exist to produce the various kinds of clefts of the lip and palate. In an extensive study of the mode of inheritance of cleft lip and cleft palate, Fogh-Andersen. I concluded that there are two different malformations with no genetic connection. In one group are clefts that involve the lip and occur most frequently in male patients. The other group is limited to clefts of the palate, which are more frequent in female patients. According to Fogh-Andersen, the manner of inheritance differs for the two groups."

3. SUBMUCOUS CLEFT PALATE

"The classic triad of diagnostic signs is the bifid uvula partial muscle separation in the midline with an intact mucosal surface, and the midline notch in the posterior edge of the bony palate. Hypernasality may or may not exist. Caution needs to be exerted prior to performing tonsillectomies and adenoidectomies because the velum may be functionally too short without the presence of the adenoid mass. Berkowitz's cephalometric and naso-pharyngoscopic studies have shown wide and unpredictable variability in the pharyngeal skeletal architecture and velar size and shape in sub mucous cleft palate as well as in all other cleft types. In some cases, due to a shallow pharyngeal space with relatively good velar length and mass with good lateral pharyngeal wall movement, no hypernasality existed. However, in most cases, the velum is usually too short, as well as too thin, and it fails to obturate the pharyngeal space properly. The problem appears to be due to an inadequate velum rather than a deficiency in lateral wall movements

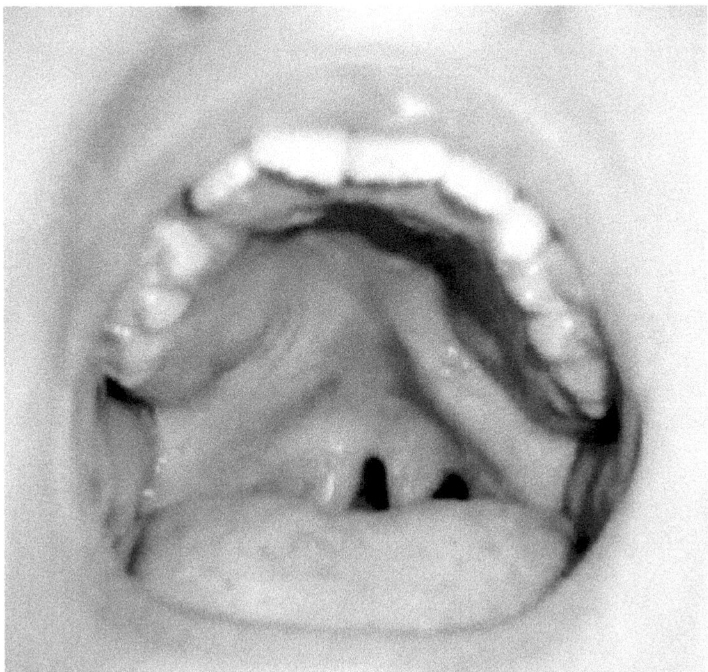

Figure 52: Submucous cleft palate. This cleft is characterized by a bifid uvula, lack of muscle continuity across the soft palate.

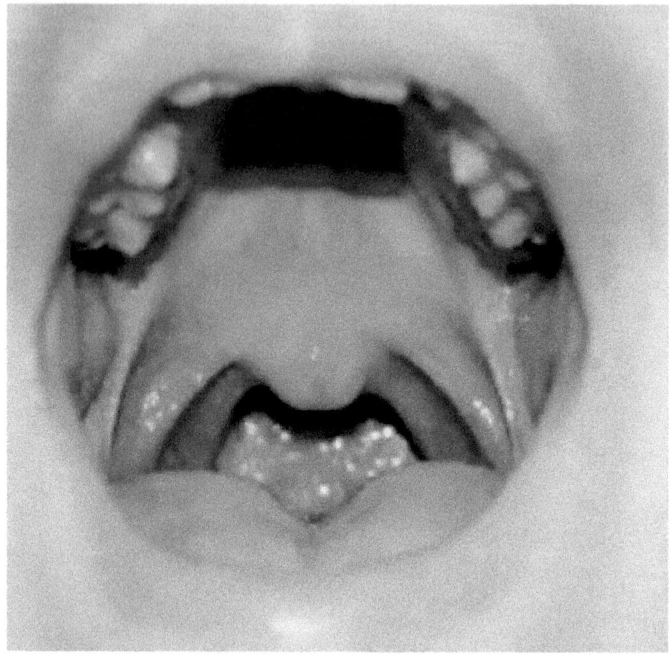

Figure 53: Submucous cleft palate. a pink zone of mucosa (zona pellucida) across the eleft in the hard palate.

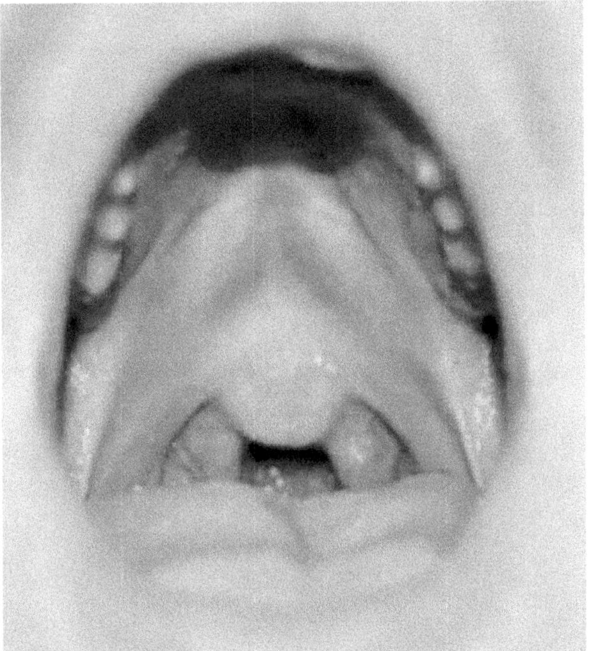

Figure 54: Submucous cleft palate. A palpable notch in the posterior border of the hard palate is always indicative of the presence of a clefter Caption

The treatment of choice is a well-positioned and adequately wide superior-based pharyngeal flap. There is no apparent need to combine a palatoplasty with the pharyngeal flap. In patients with recurring infections of the adenoids, it is recommended that the adenoids be removed before the flap is placed. Speech therapy is an integral part of postoperative management."

4. CLEFT DEFECT INCLUDING THE ALVEOLUS AND LIP.

"The alveolar portion is usually distorted outward in complete lip clefts. When the lip is united, the newly created lip force molds the alveolar section into proper alignment. A secondary alveolar bone graft is performed at the same age as in other cleft types."

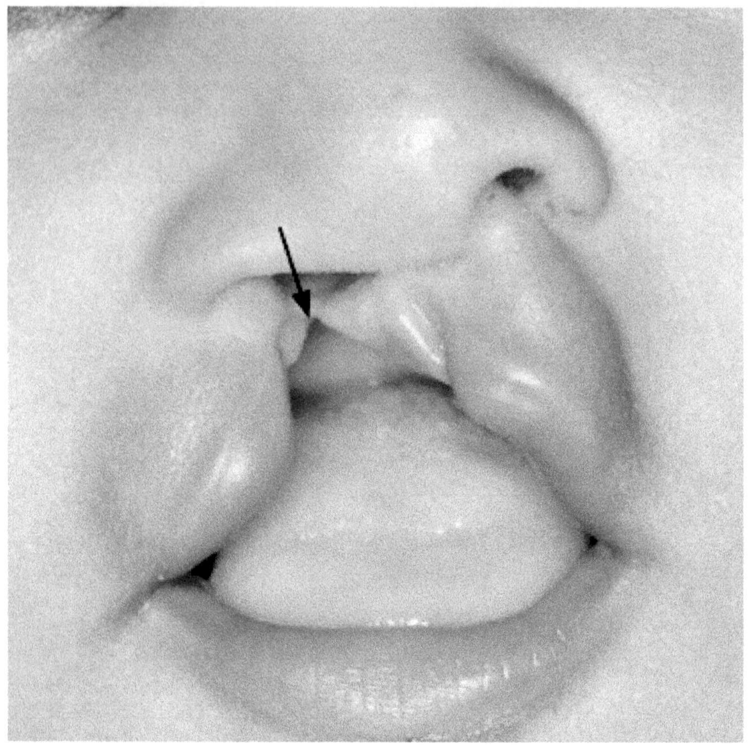

Figure 55: Cleft of the lip and alveolus.

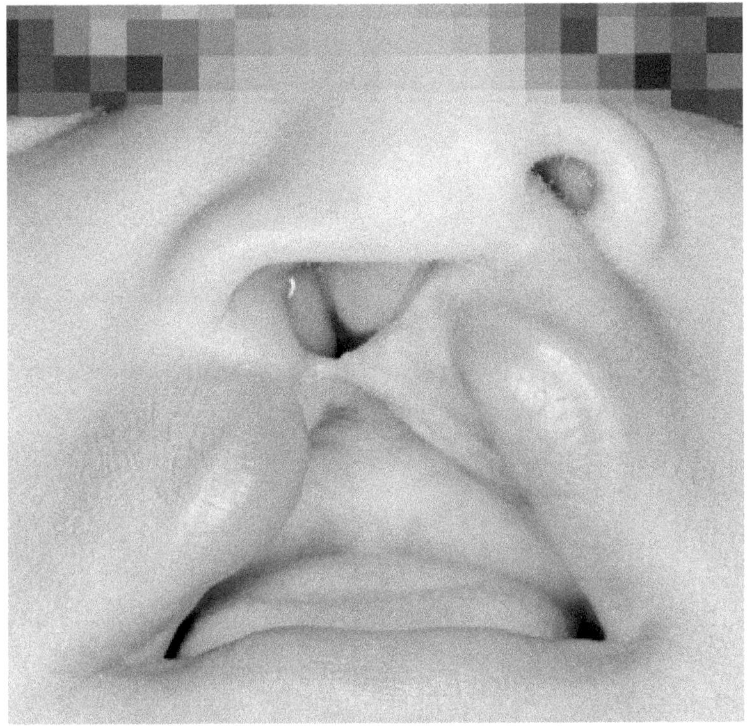

Figure 56: Cleft of the lip and alveolus.

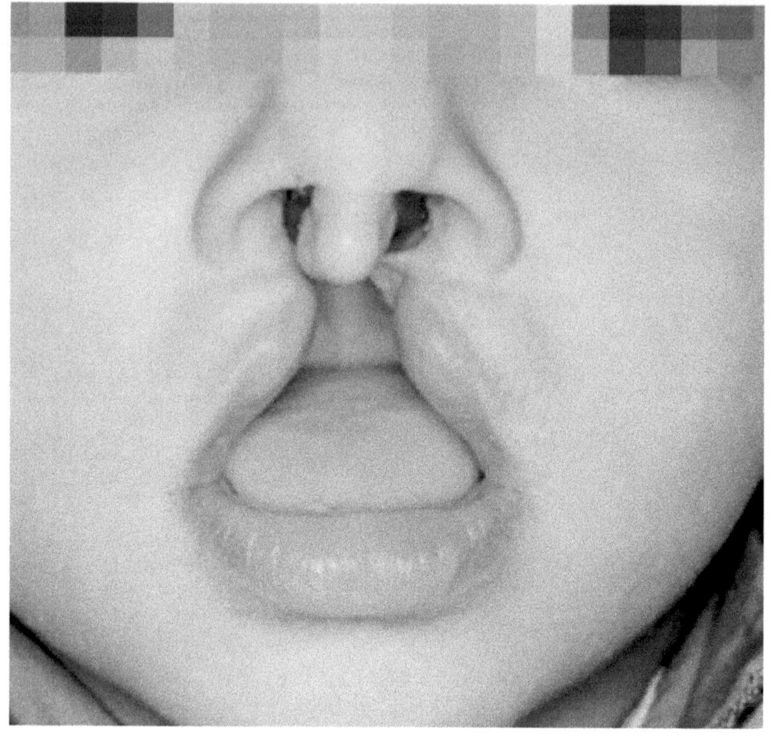

Figure 57: Cleft of the lip and alveolus.

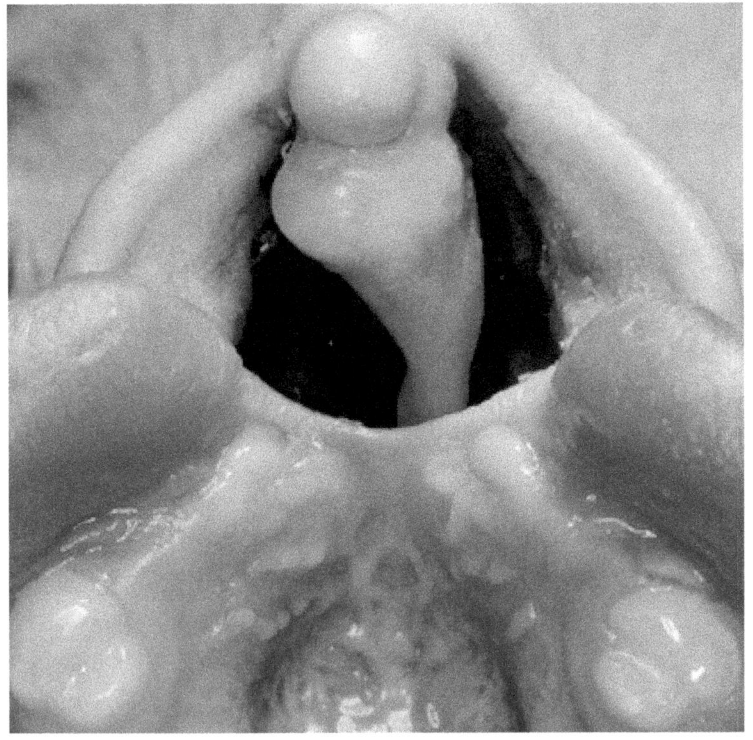

Figure 58: Cleft of the lip and alveolus.

5 AND 6.CLEFT OF UVULAE STANDING ALONE, CLEFT OF THE UVUAE INCLUDING THE UVUAE AND ALSO SOFT PALATE.

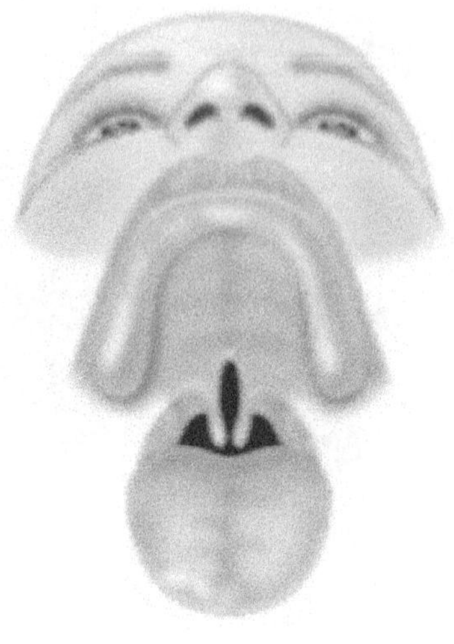

Figure 59: cleft of the soft palate (schematic diagram)

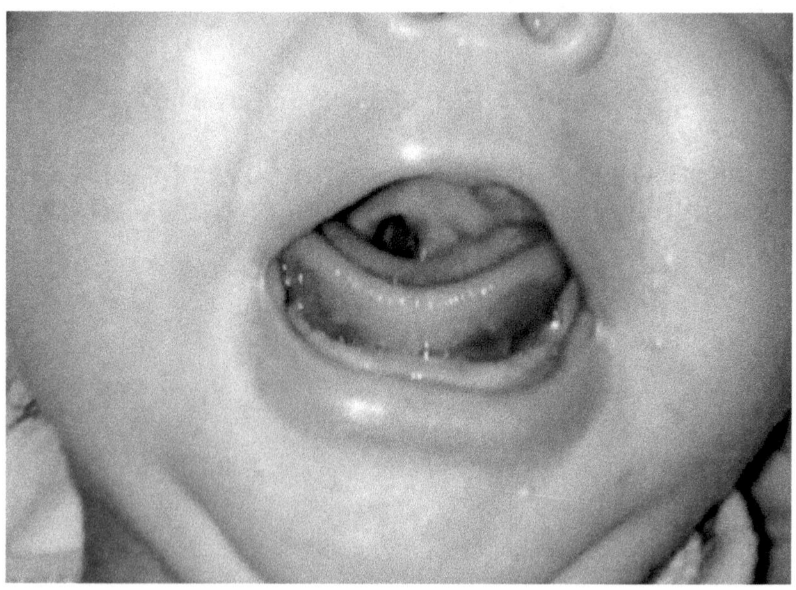

Figure 59: cleft of the soft palate

"When the health of the child permits, soft tissue clefts can be sutured within the first 3months as Latham and his mentor McNeil have suggested. There are, however, some cases when, because of an unfavourable facial growth pattern coupled with a retruded maxilla relative to the anterior cranial bases, orthopaedic protraction forces will be beneficial in the mixed (transitional) and permanent dentition."

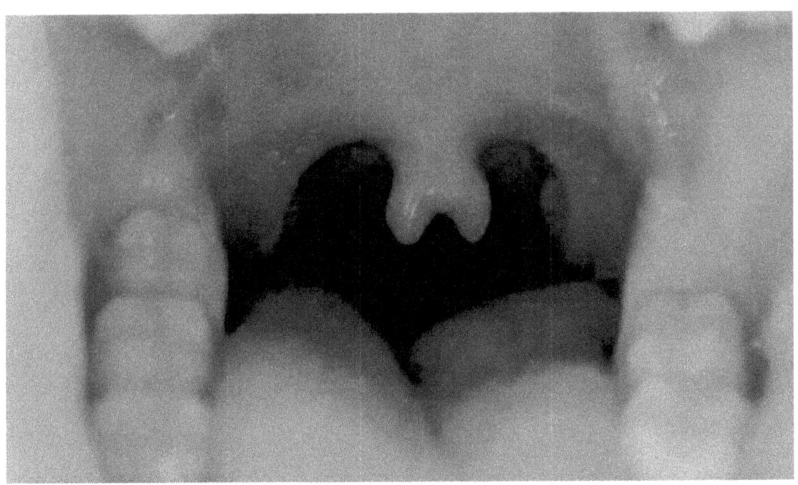

Figure 60: Cleft of bifid uvula

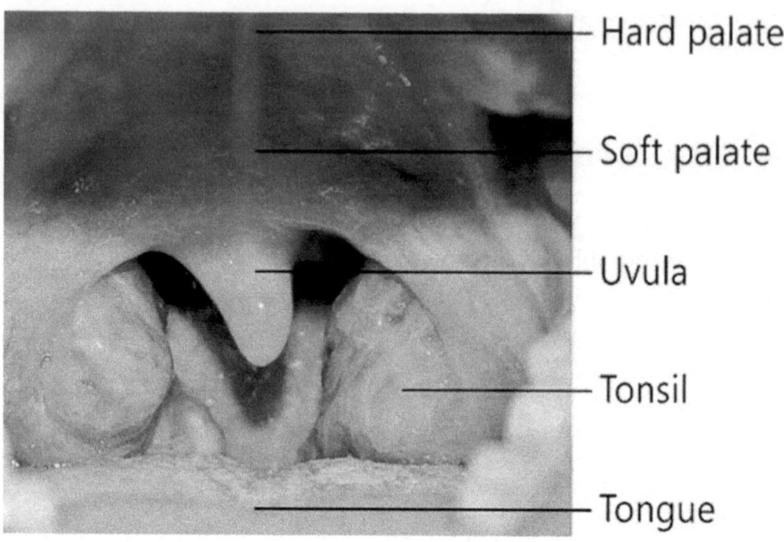

Figure 61: Cleft of Uvulae

CHAPTER EIGHT

ROLE OF PEDIATRIC DENTIST IN CLEFT LIP AND CLEFT PALATE PATIENTS

Pediatric Dentists as associates of the cleft palate team deliver support and complete healthy dentition and gums, observe craniofacial advancement and to uphold and accurate jaw relationships and dental occlusion to attain appropriate development, function and also appearance. Feeding appliances and pre-surgical infant orthopaedic decisions happen to be the most recurrently preferred by the Pediatric dentist on cleft appliance impression at most of the hospital-based curriculums. Dental care is required in situations involving congenital cleft palate, missing teeth, impaction, crowding, and delayed eruption of teeth. The oral cavity of these involved subjects is categorised by Supernumerary teeth, maxilla being affected and the mandible has an atypical shape along with the associated size. The associated dental surgeon makes efforts thoroughly in suppementation with the assigned orthodontist as well as orthopaedic surgeon to bring about time modifications of the associated oral cavity as well as the dentition. The investigators and also the members of the research committee outline two significant conclusions, them being a slight postponement of 0.96 years alongside with a steady timeline of the involved dentition also accompanied by an obvious go-slow in the process of maturity that slackens additional curiously along with increasing age.

This comprehends that the dentist must efficiently time their participation with the subjects beside these recognised restraints. They happen to invest additional efforts in the process of extraction of the recognised supernumerary teeth along with that of occurrence of impaction as well as crowding although the work being executed at varied ages as normal children.

The dentist also works thoroughly with the orthodontist and plastic surgeon to evaluate dentition all the while that the procedures are executed for approximating the alveolar ridge afterwards along with palatal closure and velo-pharyngeal port surgeries. Pre and post surgically paediatric dentist supports the patients and guardians by delivering functionally and aesthetically satisfactory occlusion, decent oral hygiene along with preventive dental care.

Examination of child with cleft at a dental set-up

The pre-eminent location in order to efficiently perceive a baby/child is characterised by its involved head being mildly depressed just onto the associated dental surgeon's lap whereas the parent or guardian occupying a position fronting the dental surgeon, assisting as well as having a control over the child's limbs including arms as well as legs. The appropriate incorporated usage of a tiny sized dental mirror is suggested.

Management of associated neonates

Neonates being victimised with a cleft palate defect end up facing trouble along the process of consumption thereby leading in great difficulty to flourish. Additionally, obstruction to the process of respiration is observed which happens to be further accredited to slightly and mandible being displaced posteriorly. This further indicates to inadequate nourishment of the involved. Reparative surgery is the current standard for management and treatment during the first year of life. At about this age or stage, the blood volume ranges between 400 and 700 ml, and the body weight varies within 5 and 10 kg. It has been seen that there is a conventional connotation amongst reduced weight of the body as well as problems involved during surgery. Thus, there is existing need for the premature intermediation through the incorporated conventional methods and ways to bring about a diminution in associated complications by bringing about an increase in weight of the body as well as lessening menace of problems in the process of surgery.

Management of the process of feeding

Parents/ Guardians should ideally be intimated to grasp and efficiently nurture the involved infant subject. When the process of feeding is commencd, the mouth as well as the palate must be appropriately prepared with the help of approximately 2-3 tsp. incorporated use of sterile water. Region nearby the neck ought to be judiciously splashed and further dried as the associated baby more frequently salivates in excess.

Subjects associated with cleft lip defect and a regular palate, infrequently exhibit any kind of trouble during the process of feeding. Subjects who have cleft palate defects, whether or not they also have cleft lip defects, sometimes trouble with eating. A cleft palate averts the infant from the creation of an approximated seal, therefore making the process unbearable for sucking of milk through the breast or bottle. Exhibits as if the subject is in the process of sucking still will be incorporating valuable calorie units in a pointless effort in acquiring satisfactory nutrition. These patients require a precision bottle and an advanced feeding technique. Useful special bottles include the Mead Johnson Bottle and the Haberman Feeder.

Methods created for specialised feeding:

The involved subjects ought be uprightly positioned. Prevention of milk from approaching through the baby's nose, is prevented by gravity. It also restricts by choking also gas, moreover reduces danger by causing infections of the middle ear. Subject must be forced in order to belch frequently. Subjects with defect of cleft palate incline towards swallowing large quantity of air all through the process of feeding even while eating while positioned upright. Ultimately time involved in the process of feeding, must be constrained approximately to 30 minutes for quantity approximated to about 2-3 ounces. Incorporated application of feeding tube being commenced advancingly in life comprises of soft-tissue perforation. The feeding tubes have seen to be assumed accountable for majority of the recognised and verified perforations, the tissues being soft primarily. followed by becoming stiff and hard soon following numerous use durations of the incorporated feeding tube, additionally producing infrequent impediments comprising of mostly perforation of the urinary bladder, perforation of the pericardial sac along with colonisation of enterobacteriaceae.

Fabrication of feeding Obturator

Formation an inflexible stage and thus leading to hindrance of the tongue in process of approaching the involved blemish, along with interfering unprompted development of the involved palatal shelves. Thus resulting in bringing about a lessened degree of nasal regurgitation including the frequency of choking. Furthermore, it complements by adding to the growth of the jaws along with the speech. Right following the obturator approximation, subject's parents and guardians require to take appropriate and efficient care of the involved appliance. Following each single time of feeding, palate needs to be ideally removed along with proper cleaning with the help of running water, followed by being soaked once in a day for about a duration of approxiately 20 min into a solution of chlorhexidine. A proper assessment of practices involved in the process of feeding presented ineffective breastfeeding along with the usage of acrylic plate being reflected accommodating by most of the involved study groups.

Infant specific Orthopaedics

In the 1950s, Burstone invented and established the relevant technology at Liverpool. Two actions are performed, the first of which is the extension of the concerned collapsed parts. The second is applying pressure to the premaxilla in order to precisely move everything in a posterior direction. This is brought about by the placement of strap made of elastic through the anteriorly placed segment that leads to application of a considerable force of contraction. In aggrevated scenarios, appliances which are pin-retained might happen to be incorporated. For a few scenarios, comprising of a specialised feeder plate along with steel wires twisted in the form of hooks further integrated along the acrylic.

Following the treatment in its active form for about a period of 3-6 weeks, it happens to be further incorporated as a retainer. Orthopaedic appliances happen to be also incorporated in order to relocate the particular segment in initial age of infancy, right before the closure of lip. They may serve as the newborns in question's "feeding plate."

Naso-alveolar Moldings

Most primary pre-surgical naso-alveolar molding appliance was developed in 1999 by Grayson et al. Naso-alveolar molding happens to be a non-surgical technique for restructuring the lip, gums and nostrils right prior to CLCP involved surgery, decreasing the involved brutality of the cleft defect. The purpose of PNAM include:

Decline in the size of the cleft by directing growth as well as functional reintegration. The continuity of the affected dental arch must be restored in order to maintain and protect oral health. Achieving optimum orientation for the cleft sections within the period of initial few months of infancy prior to the procedure of cheiloplasty. Allowing a surgically involved restoration involving negligible strain. Reduction of the protrusion of the involved alveolar processes. Preventing the tongue from appropriate seating onto the region of the cleft palatal defect, therefore simplifying transversely occurring growth of palatal shelves. Processes of molding as well as relocating the misshapening nasal cartilages. Straightening of the columella as well as alteration of alar cartilage transposition. Reduction of the necessity for secondary alveolar bone grafting. After the surgery is finished, the moulding is started, roughly 3-6 months after the baby is born.

Stage of Decidious Dentition:

Guardian or parents of individuals with cleft defects reportedly look forward to opportunities for discussion and upkeep of the patient's dental and oral development. Even before the first teeth grow, guardians often give priority to any kind of valuable information.

The key characteristics of these initial calls are as follows:

Reassurance

Information

Preventive advice

Acclimatization.

Making sure the parents understand the value of good dental and oral cavity health from the start is equally important. Establishing the most exact dental habits at a young age will assist to protect the health of both the primary and permanent dentition. Premature removal of primary teeth in individuals with cleft defects is mostly contraindicated due to potential space loss, which makes orthodontic treatment more challenging.

Considerations for preparing for and implementing good oral hygiene throughout the primary dentition stage include working with pedodontists to look for associated syndromes or sequences, like Pierre Robin's syndrome, or additional medical issues. These suggestions of any associated medical situation relative to oral care or any associated oral ailment. Young aged subjects associated with CLCP frequently have been related to middle ear contagions and subsequent auditory problems. These concerned subjects can possibly also display a considerable antiquity of recurrent sequences of antibiotic drugs for recurrent ear ailments. They may be underneath the observation of an efficient ENT surgeon and obligatory be functioned underneath the effect of general anaesthesia.

The need for general anaesthesia to undergo surgical processes could existent with a potentiality to the pediatric dentist for obligatory dental management to be executed

Hand in hand. It is obligatory to acquire complete details regarding the concerned subject's recommended prescription. It is vital for discovering the likelihood of a sugar-free substitute in these particular circumstances.

Behaviour Management

Pediatric dentist is anticipated to cross ways with definite behavioural complications. Subject showing a cleft defect might tend to be reluctant, nervous, or may have a behavioural issue. This could be accredited to recurrent hospital visits and former hospital administration might show a huge role. These involved subjects might also be predisposed by their concerned parent's behaviour which is occasionally apprehensive and domineering.

Pediatric dentist necessities endurance to create decent communication, particularly in the initial ages. It eventually demonstrates to be helpful all through the entire process of management. Pediatric dentist may also acquire speech as well as auditory problems as a shared incidence in subjects associated with cleft palate. Speech as well hearing related challenges in a subject with cleft palate might show as a conceivable blockade in developing reasonable communiqué with the involved subject. It is significant to know the patient better as a specific entity and permit him/her time aimed at essential accommodation as well as assurance build up. As conversed, it is potentially of equal vitality in order to recognise the concerned guardians, attaining their part of faith as well as assurance will help ease the delivery of consistent efficient oral care.

Preventively oriented management

Diet: Guidance to be forwarded to guardias or parents. The only dentally safe liquids that can be used in a nursing bottle are pre-boiled, then cooled with water or milk. Fruit drinks and squashes are examples of beverages with an erosive potential. Sugary and acidic drinks should be avoided at all costs and should only be drunk with meals. Children should also start using a bowl or cup for drinking when they are about six months old. Weaning involving foods as well as beverages ought be completely free from non-milk extrinsic sugars as intricately as much as permissable.

Children associated with cleft defects are frequently capable to manage with a imitation though its application is best delayed up until following the palatal repair is completely cured. The exclusion to this particular scenario is subject being associated with Pierre Robin syndrome, wherein the usage of a imitation could benefit by inspiring the reflex associated with sucking. Parents are advised to avoid comforters, including sugary beverages, especially when a child is trying to fall asleep. The mimic would ideally be not immersed in any type of food or liquid.

Although spoken dietary information should idelly continuously be delivered to parents or guardians, it is valuable to deliver them instructions in written.

Tooth brushing

Guardians might be anxious to brush in the involved area of the cleft defect, particularly resulting from primary lip as well palate related surgery. They frequently contemplate that bleeding due to gingival inflammation is instigated by injury acquired from tooth brushing or the failure of repair brought about surgically. Guardians or parents might be revealed in intricate detail about the proper procedure to brush teeth as well as gums suitably. It is noteworthy to notify the possible problematic regions of accumulation of plaque surrounding the teeth associated with cleft region. In cases where even the top part of the lip having undergone repair, worried parents should be instructed about how to elevate it by carefully broadening the lip by slither an index finger along the labial gingivae, avoiding damaging the related blemish. This ultimately helps them more by providing them a clearer view of the implicated cleft region with good contact with the related anteriorly positioned tooth crowns and the accompanying gingival margins for plaque removal. In order to properly brush a toddler, parents are advised to kneel or stand behind the child while doing so, with the head resting on the parent's torso while the chin is supported. A low-fluoride containing dentrifice comprising of not exceeding 600 ppm fluoride is suggested for subjects under the age of 6 years to diminish the probability of occurrence of enamel opacities in that of associated permanent dentition. Subjects associated with an increased danger of emerging caries should ideally incorporate use a average dentrifice (approximately 1000 ppm fluoride). Guardians or parents ought to be provided with an chance to rehearse the tooth brushing method.

Toothbrush

As a first toothbrush, a little baby brush is advised. While there is acquired overcrowding of the involved teeth or in the circumstance of an associated difficult bilateral happening cleft where its upper situated anterior might be positioned in a retroclined manner, an interdentally included brush is a beneficial additional aid. Numerous guardians being interested to give their absolute best become concerned, if at all they have challenges. Guardians of subjects with a CLCP necessitate increased sustenance, reassurance and commendation to persistence. Parental assistance and direction continue to remain as the significant portion.

Use of fluoride

Fluoride supplements:

Choices regarding implementation of fluoride complements ought to be determined by on numerous influences including the content of fluoride of the local supply of water, the probability of amenability, caries involvement of the concerned subject and their associated family members.

Fluoride varnish:

A twice timely in a year organised professional application of essential topical varnish comprising of fluoride is suggested. The greatest presentation strategy involves applying the vanish with the aid of a brush to dry tooth surfaces along with an accommodating subject.

Restorative cares for the teeth:

Restorative care is of a matter of cruciality that caries involved teeth are re-established as initially as practically conceivable. Evaluation done radiographically is essential for comprehensive management organising with regard to the carious activity as well as development. It is equally helpful to evaluate growth as well as the process of development of the involved subject. Bitewing specific radiographs ought to be measured, once the subject is capable of cooperating reasonably.

Consistent communiqué along with the cleft associated team involving the guardians of the subjects associated with cleft defect, the cleft surgeries stages are chief "Landmarks" or else "milestones." Pediatric dentist desires in order to have a considerate thoughtfulness of the surgically associated events and their concerned timing so that the oral care could be assimilated delicately all through the whole treatment stratergy. Taking an instance, the associated dentist requires to notify the concerned orthodontist regarding any appropriate dental associated treatment issue. To facilitate future orthodontic treatment planning, teeth linked to a compromised lengthy promising prognosis should be carefully considered. Any extraction due to caries should be cooperatively scheduled, especially if it necessitates using general anaesthesia to extract teeth.

Mixed Dentition Stages

The affiliated paediatric dentist plays a vital role in balancing the subject's developing uniqueness with the ongoing need for parental supervision and guidance. Various topics related to CLCP understanding challenges with school bullying On occasion, the kid subject will need psychologically related counselling, which will be arranged by concerned cleft team for the benefit of the child and the family. The augmented tendency in the direction of a Class III incisal relationship might develop additionally superficial at this particular phase. The patient as well as the family are stimulated to emphasise more on the current prominence of the inhibition of dental related ailment and also the preservation of oral related health. In a few scenarios, orthodontic treatment is commenced prematurely. Consider the possibility of delivering a straightforward upper detachable appliance to correct an anterior cross bites. When the related permanent teeth has fully emerged, conclusive orthodontic-related treatment is put into practise.

Behaviour Managements :

The patient is encouraged to start accepting responsibility for his or her own oral and dental health with anticipation serving as the main motivation. For some subjects and their worried parents or guardians, accommodating the cleft and the tooth in this particular area is frequently a big challenge. Functioning in a composed manner meticulously along with the guardian as well as child, any form of anxiety could be more easily recognised and finally overwhelmed.

Preventive Management

Dietary counselling:

With the aid of a three days diet journal, it is skillfully accomplished. Another potential problem in this age range is tooth surface loss from erosion brought on by excessive consumption of foods and beverages that are high in acid.

Tooth brushing as well as Maintenance of oral and dental hygiene

Prior to the bone grafting procedure, good hygiene should be practised because gingival irritation might cause additional bone loss. Even at this particular age and stage, a baby-sized toothbrush still is appropriate, especially when the top lip is close-fitting. Access to the teeth present through the cleft affected area is frequently problematic. An interdental brush can be used to supplement this in particular. Teeth frequently need to be brushed individually after brushing since the traditional approach of brush around the arches would remove any teeth that were oddly positioned in the affected cleft-associated region, especially those that were palatally positioned. Mouthwashes with 0.2 percent chlorhexidine gluconate are appropriate for minor episodes following surgery or to aid in stabilising gingival-related health in severe cases of gingival inflammation when the patient is fearful of the gingival tissues bleeding and is reluctant to brush.

Guidance along with tooth brushing is supportive all through the period of mixed dentition and observation is recommended until at least upto seven to eight years of age.

Pit and fissure sealant

For this particular collection of topics, fissure sealants have been given considerable thought. The process is suitably recommended for the first and second permanent molars as well as premolars, anywhere specifically designated. As soon as the teeth have started to erupt, fissure sealing should be done. sufficient to enable the occlusal surfaces' moisture to be controlled in an acceptable manner.

Use of fluorides: An applauded strategy for prevention is the effective application of fluoride varnish. If and when simply a topical effect is sought, fluoride-infused mouthwash may be utilised at this stage.

Restorative cares:

There is a chance that procedures including pulpal therapy and SSC for primary molars will be employed when appropriate.

Radiographic Managements

Numerous radiographs are required to monitor growth and development, to schedule orthodontic therapy or surgery, and to assess the outcome and stability. To assess the developing dentition and any pathophysiology, traumas or other dental conditions, radiographs may also be required.

Interceptive Cares

It is preferable to use a substitute decision for extraction of additional teeth and overly retained teeth. Altering the cross bite is also possible. In this particular worried phase, expansion of the related collapsed segment is allowed out in order to improvise the surgical approach directed to the included graft site. In the foundation of alveolar graft related, trauma occlusion is eliminated. In circumstances when a patient has a minor maxillary deficiency cleft, jaw relationship modification combining facemask therapy may be started.

Permanent Dentition Stages

This stage represents the beginning of complete orthodontic treatment. Another time, the primary responsibility of the participating dentist is to assist the patients in maintaining good oral health and avoiding dental disease.

Behaviour Management

Throughout their teenage years, subjects may experience inspiration problems and find it difficult to envision how the included orthodontic treatment will turn out. Peer pressure is strong, and school-related obligations are getting more and more difficult. Overlooked dental appointments may tend to happen. The pedodontist is in a situation to inspire and upkeep the subject in execution of the suitable precautionary processes while making the concerned conscious of the significance of being present both for orthodontic associated management as well as regular dental check-ups.

Preventive Management

Dietary oriented counselling remains to present of supreme significance.

The subject necessitates consciousness of the probable issue of decalcification surrounding the brackets placed orthodontically and also supplementary caries involved difficulties, if and when the associated frequency as well as the quantity of sugar intake is ideally not measured. Acidic rich foods as well as drinks require to be controlled to evade the likelihood of any occuring erosive damage. A 3-day constructed diet diary might be specified. Proper written guidelines, in accumulation to vocal guidance are supportive for the concerned subject to mention to when at home. A small headed toothbrush is suggested along with an interdental brush and also a twin spiral brush happens to be appreciated aids specifically for interdental usage. When fixed appliances happen to be not preferred and under the use, the incorporated usage of dental floss might be ideally suitable. Topical fluoride that has been professionally monitored and applied, most likely in the form of fluoride varnish, is still useful. Self-application of mouthwash by the patient (weekly or daily) is advised, especially during orthodontic treatment.

Restorative Cares

Dental caries-related restorations should preferably be completed prior to the start of the linked orthodontic form of treatment and usually overlooked, being maintained throughout the phase. Composite or porcelain veneers, resin-bonded bridges, and other restorative techniques based on the principle of adhesion to assist in the remodelling of the associated tooth form are included to help achieve aesthetically pleasing improvements later to the conclusion of orthodontic form of management. Conventional crowns as well as bridges or the ease of availability of a partial involved denture are often required.

Definitive orthodontic treatment

It is executed in this particular phase. The time at which orthodontic treatment should be ideally commenced remains to be a subject of conjecture. Anomalies of dental development and functional issues tend to be approached in the mixed dentition, on the other hand definitive treatment results to get procastinated till the late mixed dentition to bring about maximum growth potential along with satisfactory patient compliance. Although, few clinicians promote and prefer commencement of treatment prior in certain types of mal-occlusion:

CHAPTER NINE

PROBLEMS OF CLEFT AFFILICTED INDIVIDUALS

A cleft defect involving the alveolus could frequently have an consequence on the involved process of development for both the primary as well as permanent teeth along with the jaw. Frequently associated issues might often be associated to inherited missing of various teeth and also supernumerary teeth. The defect of cleft mostly encompasses between that of the lateral incisor as well as canine region. These particular teeth due to their close proximity to that of the cleft region, might be missing, but as and when present, they might be aggressively dislocated in order to help ease eruption into the involved margin of the cleft. These teeth also show to have a tendency to undergo morphological deformation or hypo mineralization. Although, they may tend to be reserved if at all they can furnish any kind of beneficial function in the concerned subject's wholesome dental rehabilitation. Supernumerary teeth are frequently seen, especially at the clefts margin. In an ideal world, these tooth would be removed during a specific stage of the development of the subject in question.

Commonly, supernumerary teeth associated with the permanent dentition arch is leftward to remain until an approximate of 2 to 3 months prior to bone grafting of the alveolar bone, because these teeth, although being non-functional aid in maintaining the nearby alveolar part of bone. If at all removed priorly, this particular portion of bone might tend to undergo resorption causing the alveolar cleft defect to become bigger.

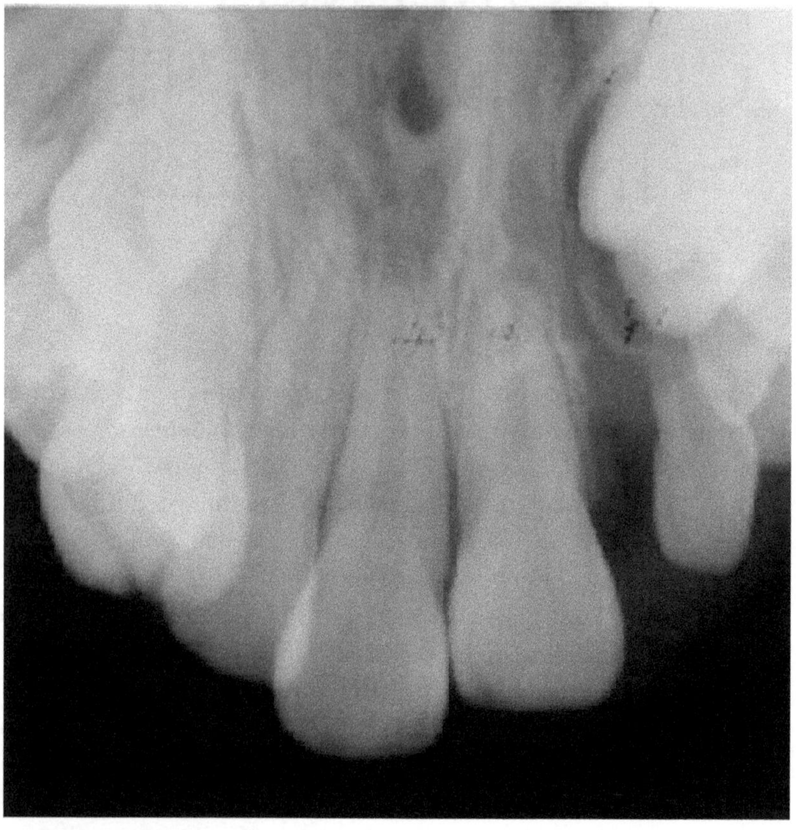

Figure 62: Oclusal radiographs from individuals with various types of cleft deformities,

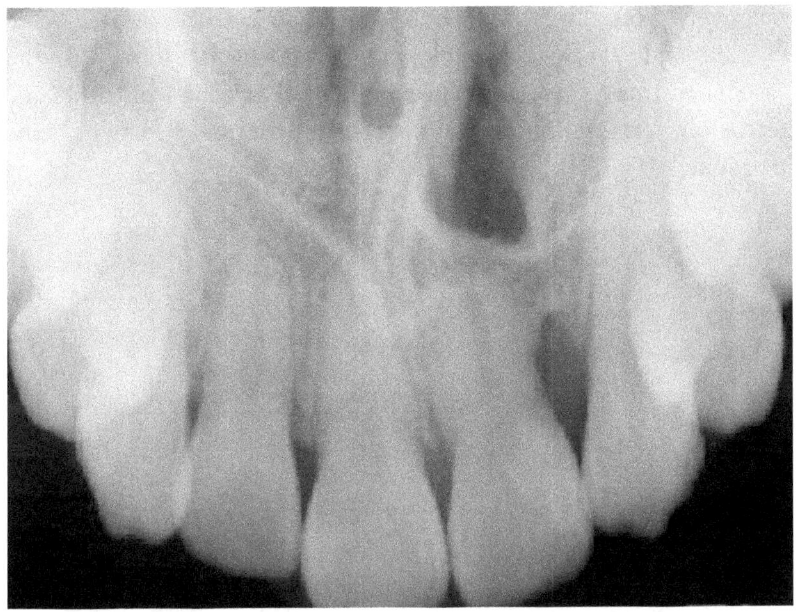

Figure 63 : Occlusal radiographs from individuals with various types of cleft deformities

Malocclusion

Folks associated with deformities associated with cleft, particularly those associated with that of the palate, tend to characterise with skeletal inconsistencies between shape, size as well as position of the jaws. Class II type of malocclusion, observed in majority of circumstances, is brought about by various influences. A frequent conclusion happens to be prognathism of the mandible, which is commonly comparative and occurs additionally due to the maxilla being retruded than by mandible being protruded. Absence or presence of extra teeth may also tend to add to the exisiting malocclusion.

Although, maxillary growth being retarded is the element which happens to be accountable for the exisiting associated malocclusion. Mostly, the operatively involved trauma caused due to the defect of cleft approximation and the resulting fibrosis (scar contracture) massively bounding the proportion of growth associated with maxilla and development.The maxilla might be limited in all associated three planes of space along with any kind of associated retrusion, constriction as well as vertical under development being frequent.

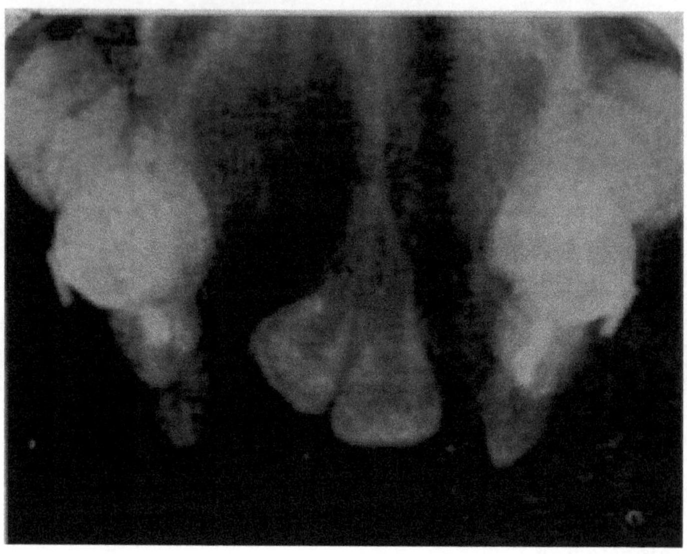

Figure 64: Bilateral complete cleft of alveolus and palate. Note absence of permanent lateral incisors

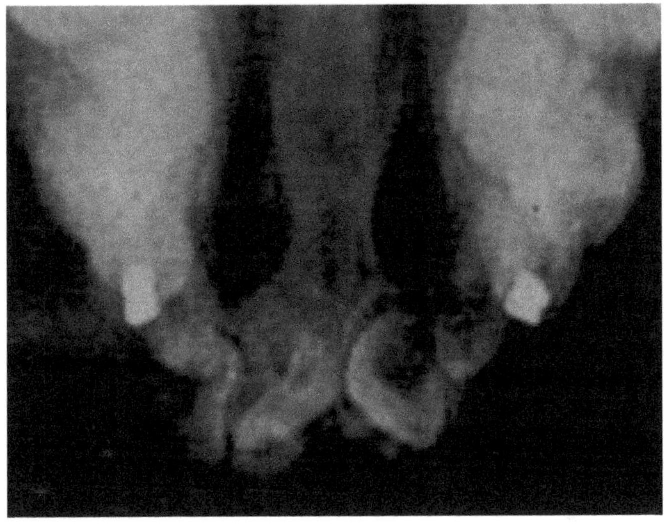

Figure 65: Bilateral complete cleft of alveolus and palate. Note absence of permanent lateral incisor on patient's left side.

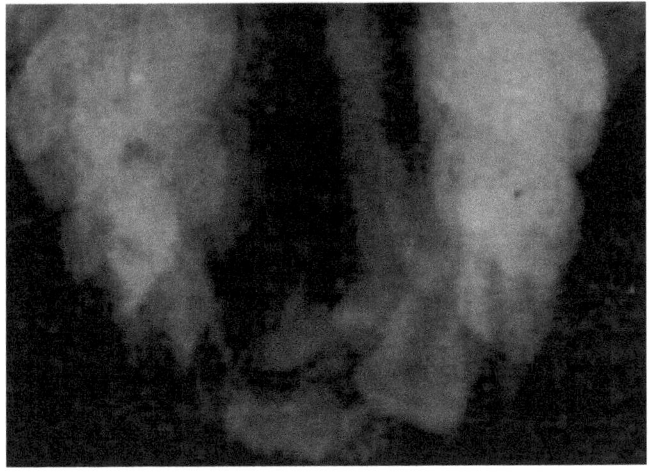

Figure 66: Unilateral complete cleft of alveolus and palate. Note. supernumerary teeth.

Unilaterally involved palatal cleft defects tend to show failure of the involved cleft defect affecting side of the maxilla towards the centre portion of the palate, this causes a narrowed dental arch. Bilateral palatal clefts typically result in the failure of all three related segments, while they can also cause the associated posterior sections to constrict and the affected anterior section to protrude. Orthodontic form of management might be seen as a necessity all through the individual's childhood and also the adolescent years.

Space maintenance and control is accommodated since the time dentiton develops. Any kind of appliance intended to uphold or upsurge the width of the associated dental arch are commonly put to use. This treatment is generally commenced along with the concerned outbreak of the first maxillary permanent molars. Wholesome orthodontically oriented care is everted until far ahead, as and when majority of the permanent teeth are erupted. Contemplation for orthognathic surgically involved intervention to bring about rectification and management of skeletal related deformities and occlusally related disharmonies is often required at the particular time.

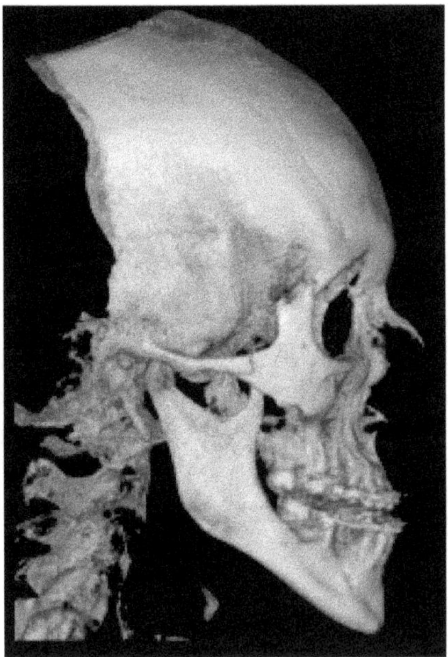

Figure 67: A, facial profile of typical cleft patient. Note pseudoprognathic appearance of mandible.

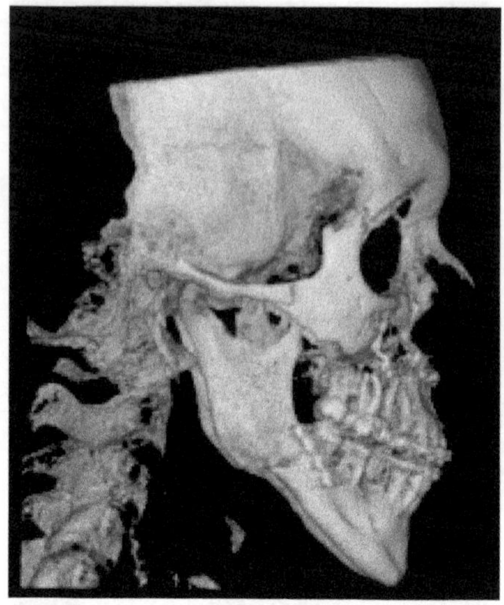

Figure 68: Occlusal relationship of patient showing Angle's ClassIII relationship.

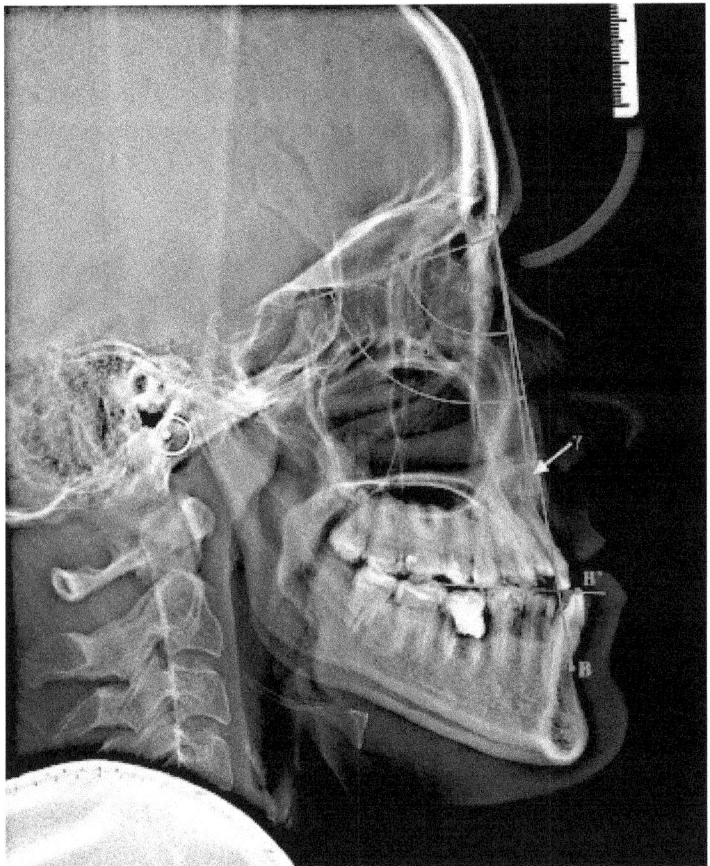

Figure 69: Lateral cephalagram showing maxillary skeletal sagittal deficiency contributing to Class of occlusal relationship

Nasal Deformities

People with cleft lip defects frequently exhibit deformity of the accompanying normal anatomy of the nose. The alar cartilage on the same side tends to get flared and the columella of the nose is then pulled toward the non-cleft involvement side if and when the cleft defect tends to spread onto the floor of the involved nose. The current problem is complicated by a primary bone support that is inadequate for the base of the nose. Until all cleft defects and their related problems are resolved, surgically altering nasal-related deformities should generally be postponed. This is because doing so tends to correct the associated alveolar cleft defect, and doing so will alter the osseous-related foundation of the nose. This results in increased deviations in the associated form of the nose. As a result, the cleft patient may require a nasal revision as their final corrective surgical procedure.

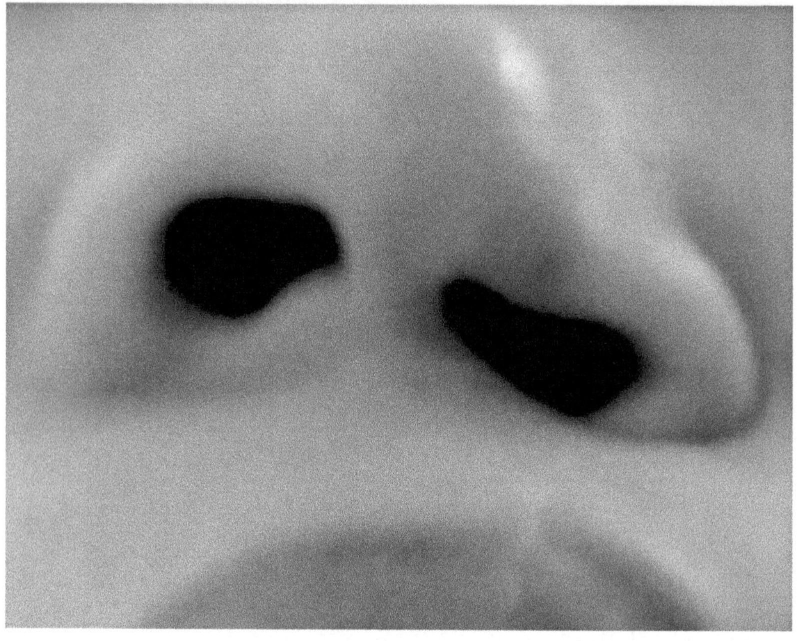

Figure 70: various types of Nasal Deformities, Nasal deformities are also apparent. Unilateral complete cleft of lip and palate.

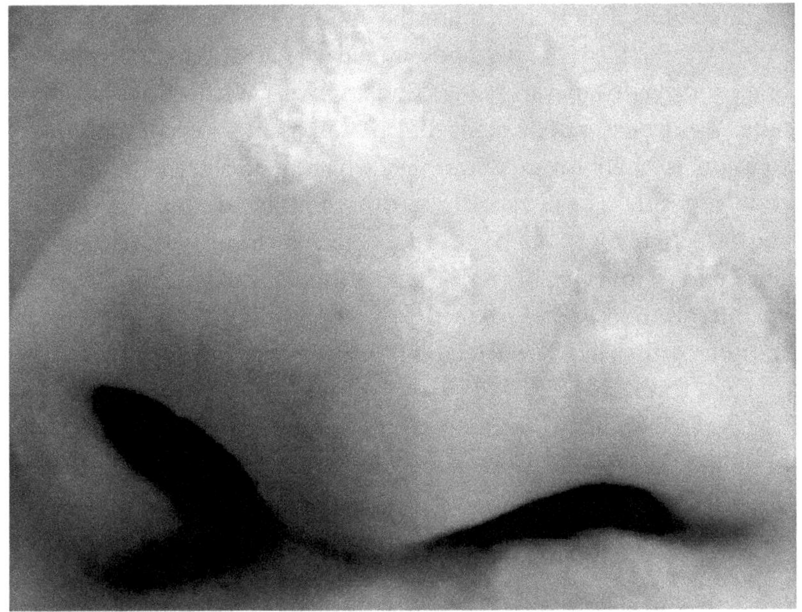

Figure 71: various types of Nasal Deformities, Nasal deformities are also apparent. Bilateral complete cleft lip and palate.

Feeding

Children with cleft palatal abnormalities are able to swallow normally when the food they are eating reaches the nasopharynx, but it is difficult for them to create the necessary negative pressure in their mouths to help them when sucking breast milk or bottle milk. The sucking and swallowing reflexes are thought to be normal because they are triggered whenever a nipple is placed in the subject's mouth and they begin to suck. Although, the musculature being undeveloped or improperly positioned in order to cause the sucking relfex to be effecient. This particular issue is effortlessly overcomed by incorporating the usage of particularly intended nipples which are characterised to be elongated as well as seen to spread additionally further into that of the child's mouth. The opening ought be distended, due to the process of sucking not being as efficient as that seen in a normal child.

Apart than these, methods aimed at satisfaction include the usage of eyedroppers or any kind of large syringes with rubber tubes being extended, being linked to them. A small amount of solution is then injected through this specific catheter into the child's mouth. These specific feeding methods require more time and effective care, yet being adequate for those with the means. The child is not typically fed when reclining or when more frequent burping is necessary since the infant swallows an appropriate amount of air when these feeding techniques are used.

Ear Problems

People who have a soft palate cleft deformity are more likely to have middle ear infections. Reviewing the complex arrangement of the soft palate's levator veli palatini and tensor veli palatini muscles, which are frequently added to the same group of muscles on the opposing side and are then left free when the soft part of the palate has a cleft defect, makes the justification clearer and more obvious. These particular musculature have their roots either straight on or from close to the auditory tube. These particular muscles bring about foundation of the ostium of this particular tube onto that of the nasopharynx. This specific act is generated as and when middle ear pressures are synchronised by swallowing during changes in atmospheric pressure, such as through rising or descending on an aeroplane. The related middle ear develops a sealed area when a certain action is discontinued or altered and is devoid of any drainage mechanism.

Serous fluid might then get accumulated which would further consequence in serous otitis media. Must microbes locate their approach from that of the nasopharynx into the part of the middle ear, a contagion may tend to grow. In order to make troubles more downgrade the auditory tube to be placed in infants is at a specific angle that does not allow or facilitate any dependent drainage. As people age, their angulation changes, making them more dependent on middle ear drainage.

People with cleft palate defects frequently need to have a portion of their middle ear "vented." This procedure is carried out by the oto-rhino-laryngologist, who ends up making a hole through the inferior portion of the eardrum and inserting a little tube made of tubing. The ear ultimately empties into the outside rather than the nasopharynx (myringotomy).

Infants with cleft palate and numerous myringolomics arch are more likely to have chronic serous otitis media. Due to the ongoing middle ear inflammation caused by chronic serous otitis media, there is a known risk to the audible range. Cleft palate patients frequently experience hearing loss. The patient with the cleft defect of the palate experiences conductive audible range loss, which means that neural type of pathway to the brain continues to function as it did previously or normally. In these specific cases, the only defect or deformity is that sound cannot adequately reach the auditory related sensory organ due to chronic inflammatory changes in the middle ear. However, if and when the problem is not identified and treated, it is also possible for the auditory related sensory nerves to sustain lasting harm. It becomes challenging to fix this specific type of damage.

People with cleft palate deformities exhibit a wide range of hearing loss. If the loudness drops significantly enough, normal-sounding speech might be heard at less than half of the typical volume. Additionally, phonemes—clear spoken sounds—may not always be recognised accurately, as in the case of sounds like st and sh. In order to assess the hearing ability and performance in persons with cleft palates, audiograms are helpful instruments that are frequently used.

Speech Difficulty:

The malformation associated with cleft lip and cleft palate typically results in four speech-related problems. The most common observation is that there is a decline in consonant sounds like b, I d, and k. g. Because the expansion of basic terminology depends on consonant sounds, more language-related activity is expanding. Resulting in decent auditory judgement is deficient through the time the associated palate is approximated. When a patient has a soft palate cleft defect, hyper nasality is frequently present and persists even after surgically induced correction. Dental related deformity, mal-occlusion and irregular placement of tongue might advance prior to the closure of the associated palate and therefore brings about a problem related to articulation. Hearing related complications contribute massively to various ailments relatet to speech frequent in subjects with those of oral cleft defects.

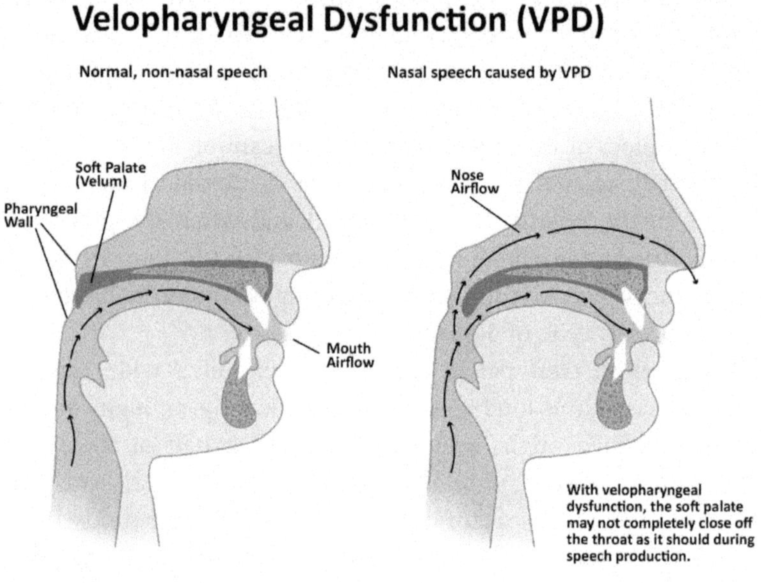

Figure 72: Upward and backward movement of soft palate during normal speech. Its contact with posterior pharyngeal wall is shown

The following approach is used to show how speech develops in any typical single. The lungs serve as the source from which air is forced out, passing through the linked voice cords on the way to the concerned mouth cavity. Speech sounds are produced by the precise alignment and positioning of the tongue, lips, lower jaw, and soft palate when they work in unison in an incredibly synchronised manner. The voice would be superimposed on speech sounds as a result of the prevalent association of the structure present inside the mouth cavity if and then when the vocal cord were placed into perfect vibration while the airstream was forced to pass between. The associated soft part of palate is elevated throughout production the speech, averting the escape of air through that of the nose. It is required for the person in question to have adequate limitation of the air channel from the oropharynx to since the nasopharynx in order to achieve clear speech. The linked nasal and oral cavities are divided by the hard portion of the palate.

The soft portion of the palate often functions as a crucial valve to stop the flow of escape air between the oropharynx and nasopharynx. Another name for this is the velo-pharyngeal mechanism. The soft palate as well as the pharyngeal walls are its two main parts, as the name implies. When not in use, the soft part of the palate hangs down, facing the part of the tongue. However, when speaking, the soft part of the palate is elevated and drawn toward the back of the associated pharyngeal wall, which is what happens to the soft part of the palate in a typical person when they are instructed to say "ah." in usual speech this particular act undergoes speedingly along with an unrealistic intricacy, so that the mechanism associated with valving tends to allow big quantities of air to outflow into that of the part of nasopharynx or could cut down the spurt to none.

The mechanism connected to the velopharyngeal component does not function in subjects with soft palates who have a cleft defect because there is a break in the musculature that runs from one side to the other. As a result, the soft palate portion does not elevate to make contact with the pharyngeal wall portion. This constant airflow into the nasal cavity has the effect of making speech sound more nasal, or hyper-nasal. Subjects with defects of cleft palate tend to get established supplemental velopharyngeal, tongue aslo nasal mechanisms in a try to establish understandable speech. The parts of posterior as well as lateral pharyngeal walls acquire appropriate flexibility and then endeavour to constrict the passageway between that of the oropharynx as well as nasopharynx while making speech. In a few individuals with both the abnormality of cleft palate, an accompanying muscular kind of pharyngeal wall bulge develops during the efforts at sealing the associated channel and is started referring to it as Passavant's ridge rather than bar. Subjects with cleft palate anomalies often adopt compensatory tongue and body positions, while speaking helps to help valve the air entering from of the larynx and finally enter the pharyngeal-related areas. Just like that flic apparent group of musculature surrounding the nose associated with expressions of the face are involved to aid in curbing the volume of escaping air from that of the nasal cavity. In this specific case, the velo-pharyngeal mechanism is used to valvulate the nasal cavity on the opposite side. Although, for an uncorrected cleft defect of the soft part of palate, it is very challenging for compensatory tools to establish a appropriate velo-pharyngeal mechanism. Sadly, in surgically brought about correction of the soft part of palates, velopharyngeal capability is not frequently attained with just one time of operation thus making secondary procedures necessary.

Speech pathologists have extensive experience helping people with cleft-related abnormalities develop normal articulation abilities. Subjects with cleft-related abnormalities start receiving training for speaking earlier in life. Subjects might require to attend speech oriented counselling for multiple years in order to produce satisfactory and appropriate speech. The hearing associated challenges are also observed. Auditory loss at a primary age is particularly damaging to the establishment of regular speech skills. Subject who is unable to hear is incapable to duplicate standard speech. Therefore, parents should be aware of their worried child's developmental status and ensure that regular doctor appointments are made.

Associated Anomaly

Although a subjects with an oral related cleft defect is roughly 20 times more likely than a normal child to experience another associated inherited irregularity, there is no clear correlation with specific anatomic areas of additional anomaly involvement of those who have related irregularities. "S8% have isolated cleft invovling palate and 21% have cleft lip even without cleft palate," the study found. In the overall cleft-afflicted population. Approximately 30% have other anomalies in addition to the facial cleft, ranging from neurologic disturbances of every clef-afflicted population. 10% have congenital heart disease and 10% have some degree of mental retardation. Thus, the child with a facial cleft may require additional care beyond the scope of the cleft team."

CHAPTER TEN

DIAGNOSIS

Occasionally cleft defects are analysed with the help of prenatal ultra sound, altough there is absence of screening for oral-facial clefts in a systematic way. More commonly oro-facial clefts are identified right following the birth of the child. Nevertheless, occasionally minor form of cleft defects might be unable to be identified until late. Cleft lip can be effortlessly identified by execution of ultrasonography during the second phase or trimester of pregnancy, right when the location of face of the fetus is aligned properly.

Prenatally orientd diagnosis offers guardians the benefits of consuming time in order to formulate psychologically for that of the birth and expand their information regarding the birth defect. Along with enhancements in the determination of the involved equipments as well as techniques used for ultrasound, craniofacial associated deformities of the fetus are currently fortunately recognisable. Oral clefts happen to be commonly occurring facial defect. The prenatal analysis of facial defect of clefts permits for satisfactory advising as well as preparation for prenatal oriented care as well as delivery.

The method to make prompt diagnosis of the defects of cleft lip and palate seems to be documented as the two associated planes of the face of the fetus being acquired. As in recognised frontal plane, it is possible to identify a disturbance of a normal mid-facial architecture and the absence of the maxillary ridge to some extent anteriorly and inferiory lto the orbits. Additionally, an illustration of the corresponding nasal cavity's enlargement is provided. An anteriorly protruding soft tissue mass is visible in the recognisable coronal plane, directly beneath the midpoint of the nasal septum, where the nose is visible. An extensive survey focused on anatomy is justified whenever an oral cleft abnormality has been detected by ultrasonography because there are over 350 disorders, including even chromosomal anomalies, that can accompany clefting of the face.

"Nyberg et al suggest an ultrasound classification for oral clefts which describes five types

Type I includes an isolated cleft lip without palate, Type 2 includes unilateral cleft lip and palate. Type 3 is bilateral cleft lip and palate. Type 4 is the median cleft. Type 5 refers to clefts associated with amniotic bands or limb-body-wall complex. The detection rate for prenatal diagnosis of oral clefts is dependent on factors such as the experience of the operator, indications for the studies, i.e., risk factors, and gestational age at the time of the study. In addition in some prenatal ultrasound laboratories, this is not done. Examination of the fetal face in not currently included in the guidelines for performance of the ante-partrum obstetrical ultrasonographic valuation published by the American Institute of Ultrasound in Medicine.

Clementi et al. reported the experience in the detection of oral cleft in

20 European countries. Most of the participating countries, evaluation of the fetal face was done routinely. Out of 709,027 births, there were 751 facial clefts (1 per 1000); 553 were cleft lips with or without palate and 198 were isolated cleft palate. The detection rate was 27% for cleft lip/palate and 7% for cleft palate. Fetal deaths occurred in 4% of the cases.

On the other hand, Brenshtein et al. reported their experience on early detection by trans-vaginal ultrasound. The population included 14,988 trans-vaginal ultrasounds performed during the 12 to 16 weeks of gestation; 25% of the population was low risk for oral clefts and 75% had risk factors. The incidence of oral clefts was 0.8 per 1,000 (12 cases) and the detection rate was 92% (11/12). Even in experienced hands, ultrasound has its limitations in correctly identifying the involvement of the palate. Cash and Coleman studied the detection rate in low risk population in the United Kingdom, where the fetal face is routinely evaluated , There were 30 cases of oral cleft in a population of 23,577 (1.3 per 1,000). The detection rate for cleft lip and palate was 93% (13/14), 22% (2/9) for isolated cleft palate, and 67% (2/3) for isolated Cleft lip. There were no cases of false positive diagnosis. The overall detection rate was 65% and the correct diagnosis was made in 71% of cases. There is also the concern about false positive diagnosis of oral clefts.

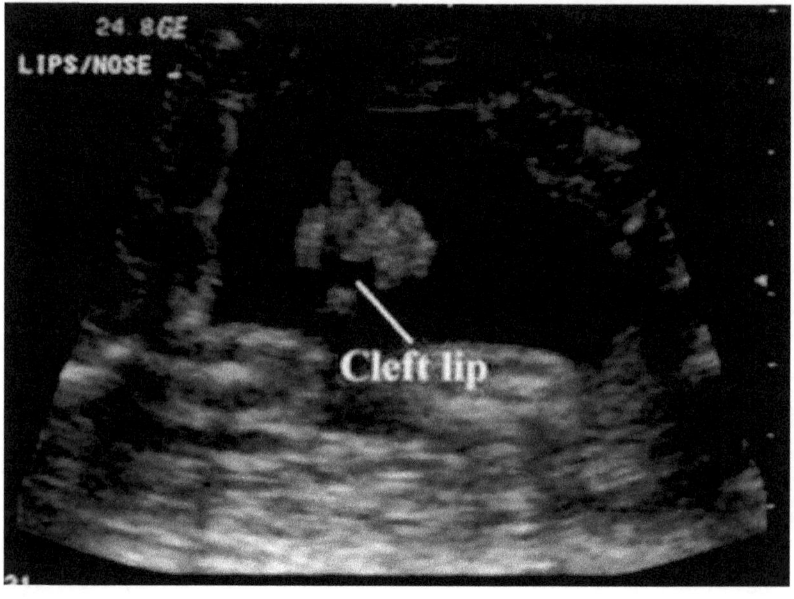

Figure 73: Transvaginal Ultrasound of Cleft lip

Hafner et al performed prenatal ultrasound to detect malformations of the fetal face in 5,407 women. There were clefts identified, 8/11 (72%) were detected prenatally. However, there were 8 false positive cases for 99.8% specificity.

It was interesting in this study that there was a 100% detection rate when the oral cleft was associated with other fetal anomalies, but 50% when it was isolated. Gestational age at time of the ultrasound has implications in the ability to detect oral clefts.

Robinson et al. reported their experience in Brigham and Women's Hospital. There were 56 Confirmed cases of cleft lip in a period of 10 years. The detection rate was 57% before 20 weeks of gestation versus 80% when the ultrasound was done after 20 weeks. Therefore, in patients at increased risk for oral clefts and with a normal early ultrasound should have a repeated study after 20 weeks of gestation. Three dimensional ultrasound seems to aid in the correct diagnosis of oral clefts.

Chen et al. evaluated 21 fetuses with confirmed oral clefts scanned between 20 to 34 weeks of gestation. The accuracy (true positive +true negative) of 3D ultrasound in the diagnosis of oral clefts was 100% versus 29% for 2D ultrasound. In another study by Chmait et al., they found a 100% accuracy of 3D ultrasound versus 91% for 2D ultrasound. However, the same study found a decreased specificity for cleft palate with 3D ultrasound (83%) versus 2D ultrasound (92%). Neonates with cleft lip/palate usually do not have associated malformations. However, the incidence of severe structural anomalies, mainly central nervous system and cardiac, detected by prenatal ultrasound in association with oral clefts is increased. This is due to a high incidence of fetal demise and elective termination of pregnancy.

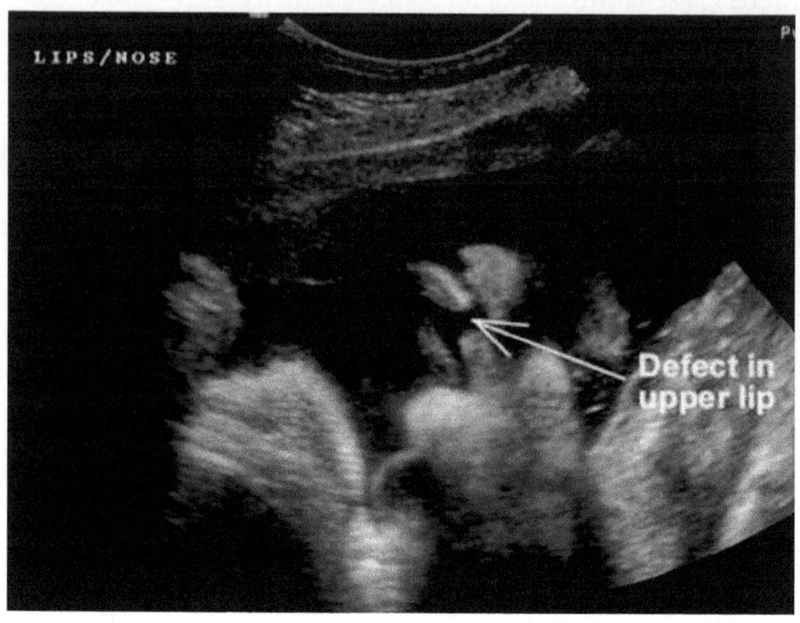

Figure 74: Unilateral cleft lip

Saltzman et al. found that 10 out of 12 cases (83%) of fetuses with

Prenatally diagnosed oral clefts had other structural anomalies, and 4 out of the 10 (40%) had an autosomal trisomy.

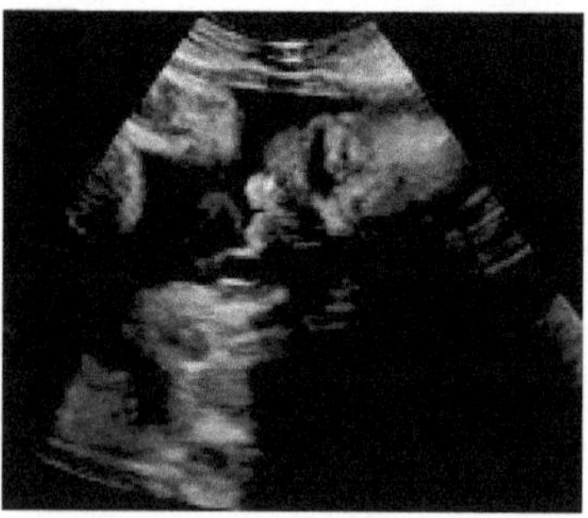

Figure 75: Bilateral Cleft lip and palate

Benacerrafet al. described the outcome of 32 fetuses with prenatally diagnosed oral cleft. Out of 32 fetus diagnosed over a 3 ½ year period as having cleft lip or palate by ultrasonography examination. 53% (17/32) had other sonographically detected structural abnormalities. 35% of these (6/17) had an aneuploidy, (5 had trisomy 13 and 1 had trisomy 18). The five pregnancies were electively terminated, 8 died in-utero or in the neonatal period. Of the 15 fetuses that had no abnormalities detected 47% (Four electively terminated (27%), one miscarried, and one had vertebral abnormalities and died due to pulmonic stenosis. Nine survived (60%) and underwent successful correction of their cleft lip/palate.

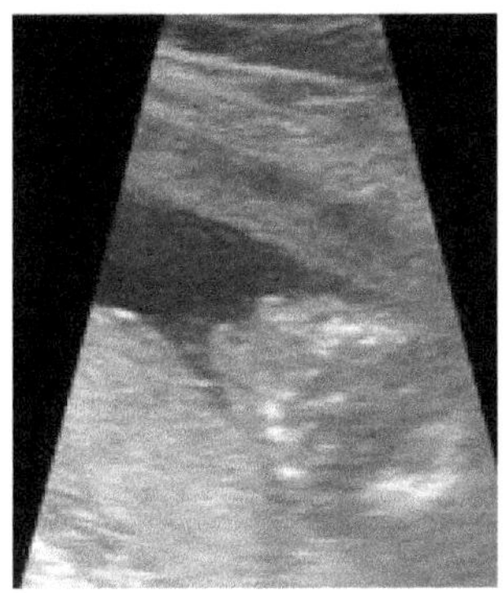

Figure 76: Bilateral Cleft lip and palate

Nicolaides et al. found that all the fetuses diagnosed with oral clefts and chromosomal abnormalities had associated structural anomalies. Nyberg et al. reported on the correlation of type of cleft with chromosomal abnormalities and associated structural anomalies. They found a risk of 0% for chromosomal abnormalities and 20% for associated structural malformations in Type (unilateral cleft lip); 20% and 47% respectively for Type 2 (unilateral cleft lip and palate), 30% and 55% respectively for Type 3 (bilateral cleft lip and palate); 52% and 100% respectively for Type 4 (median cleft). There was only one fetus with a chromosomal abnormality and isolated oral cleft.

Berge et al. found that the risk for chromosomal abnormalities, other structural fetal anomalies, and fetal death was 0%, and 0% respectively. For Type 1; 32%, 48%, and 48% respectively. For Type 2: 0, 72%, and 65% respectively for Type 3; 82%, 100%, and 100% for Type 4.

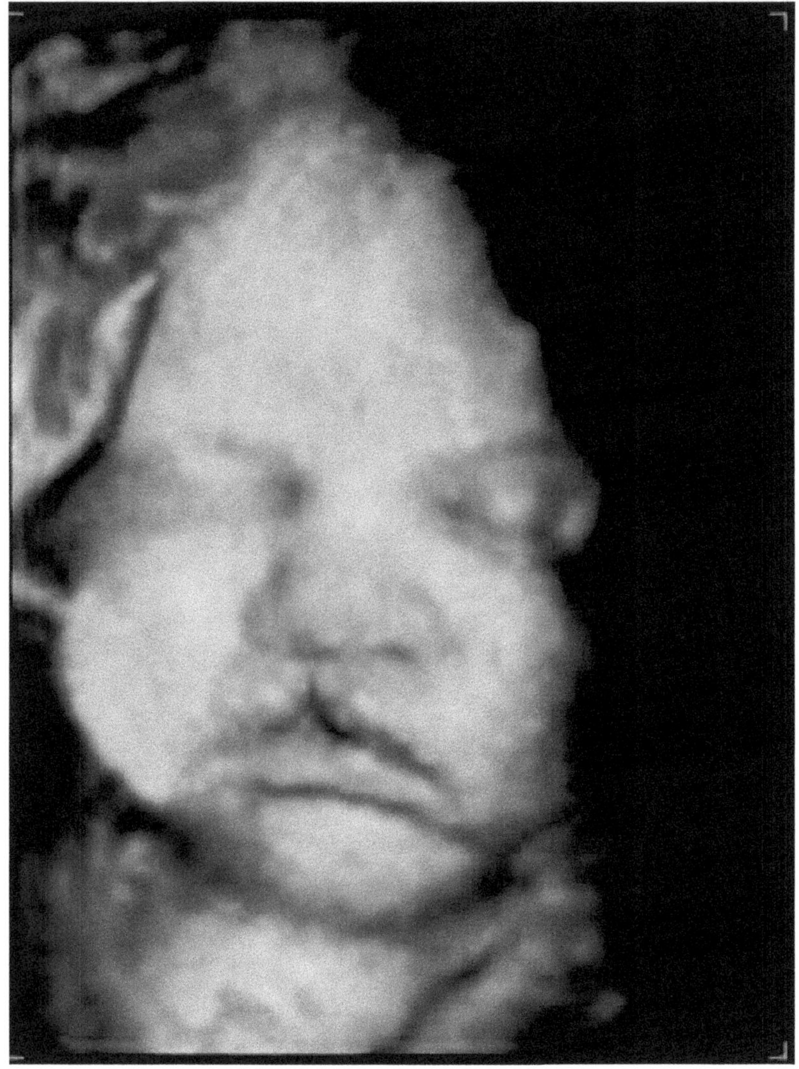

Figure 77: Unilateral cleft lip

Fetuses with isolated cleft palate had abnormal chromosomes, other malformations and died in utero or in the neonatal period. Prenatal diagnosis of oral cleft is important for those parents at increased risk for recurrence. Ultrasound laboratories that routinely perform evaluation of the fetal face have to be familiar with limitations of the diagnosis, i.e., accuracy of the diagnosis and false positive results.

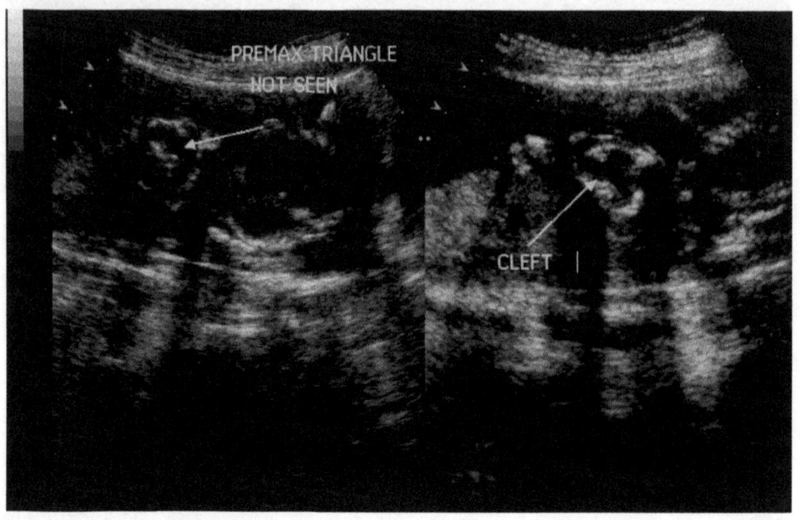

Figure 78: Bilateral Cleft lip and palate

Also, these laboratories should be prepared to offer adequate counselling and referral to experts in the treatment and correction of oral clefts. Amniocentesis for isolated oral clefts remains unresolved with incidence of aneuploidy reported to be as low 0% to as high as 5%. Proponents of routine visualization of the fetal face argue that the future when fetal surgery becomes safer for both mother and fetus, foetuses with oral cleft may benefit from early in utero intervention."

CHAPTER ELEVEN

MANAGEMENT

Birth abnormalities that are common and treatable include facial clefts (OFCs). Orofacial clefts have a variety of etiologies, including multifactorial, environmental, and hereditary causes. Delivering comprehensive preventive and maintaining oral health care is a dentist's role in managing people having cleft and craniofacial defects. The dentist frequently needs to collaborate with a team of specialists due to the diversity of surgical procedures required to rehabilitate patients with facial clefts. To achieve the best possible health results for those affected, various facilities' practises, their involvements, and their timeliness are of utmost importance. With the primary goal of providing the greatest care and improving their quality of life, patients will be managed from the time of birth until they reach adulthood.

Management of New borns with OFC

A paediatric consultation, genetic testing, feeding instructions, and counselling should all be scheduled for the newborn soon after birth. While still in the hospital, the newborn must undergo a hearing test, and a cleft evaluation is also performed.

Lip taping can begin close to where the broad cleft begins. In a typically developing infant, the American Cleft Palate Craniofacial Association advises correcting the cleft involving defects by the age of 18 months. The scheduling of palate repair must take into account both the likelihood of speech impairment if the repair is carried out too late and the likelihood of disrupting the normal craniofacial if carried out too early. To reduce the likelihood of velo-pharyngeal inadequacy, that has been shown to increase, several organisations that deal with clefts recommend before correction.

Alveolar Nasal Molding (NAM)

The interdisciplinary team's ability to improvise and preserve adequate naso-labial aesthetics while doing initial lip or nasal surgery on infants with oro-facial clefts has substantially improved thanks to NAM. Infants should be assessed as soon as is practical, ideally during the first 2 weeks of life. The infant is evaluated to check for any breathing issues and to confirm that he or she is in good health before the orthodontist/dentist takes an imprint of the maxillary arch using an acrylic resin impression tray that is somewhat bigger in scale than the maxillary arch. This was selected from the a collections of custom-made tray of different sized that were constructed from previously-purchased maxillary dental casts. After obtaining the impressions, a stone cast of the impression is created and replicated. The second cast is used to create the appliance, while the first cast is maintained for the patient's paperwork. A palatal plate made of resin that has been light-cured or thermocured is next inserted, followed by the modified nasal stent. The day of delivery, the device is put near to the upper arch; a delicate loop is then attached to the distal end of the wire; and last, a small amount of light-cured glue is applied to a nasal stent's tip. Parents are given comprehensive information and instructions about where to put the device, how to remove it from the case, or how to take care of it after it gets habituated. They are also instructed to look out for symptoms of prosthesis-related discomfort.

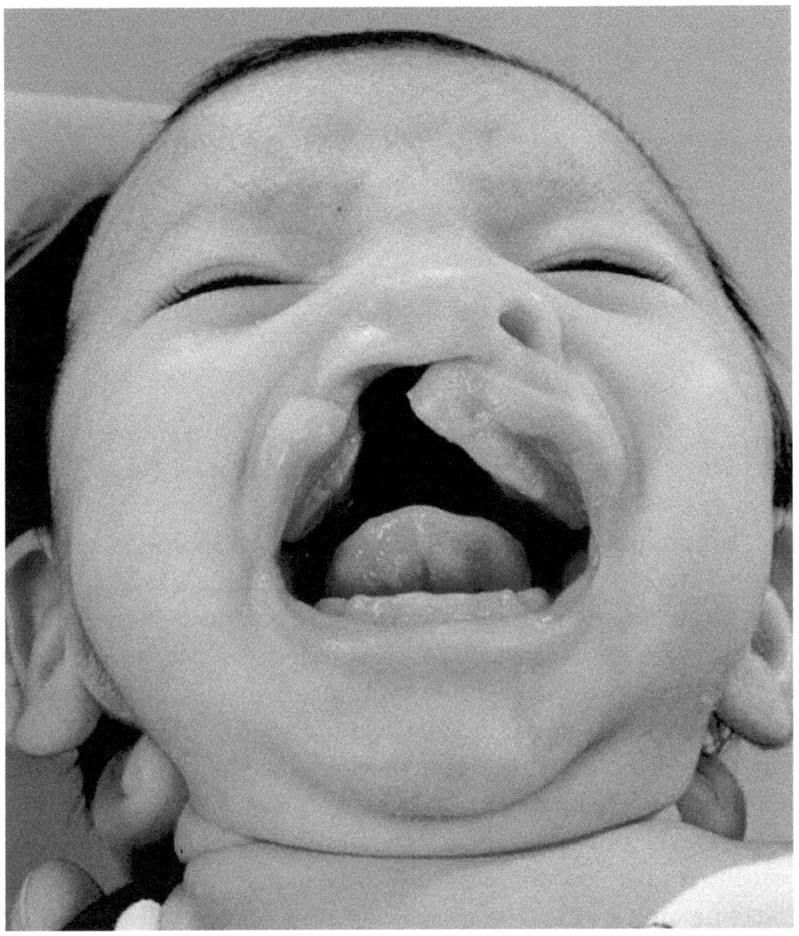

Figure 79: A 2-week old child with bilateral complete cleft lip and palate.

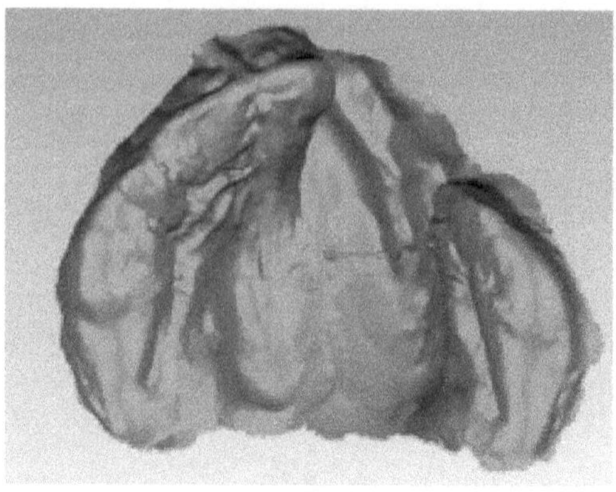

Figure 80: Impression in preparation for NAM

Denture paste adhesive is used to keep the appliance in place. Once a week, the patients are observed for changes, and both the nasal and alveoli mouldings begin at same time. The molding pressure also on nasal cartilage is readjusted, the alveolar segments are directed to realign, and improvements in comfort are made. The three main goals are to advance the apex of the anterolateral cartilage to the tip of the nose, prolong the short columella, and keep the morphological changes which have already been done. The appliances is worn constantly up until the time of cleft lip surgery, which normally occurs at three or four months of age, apart from cleaning after meals. The progress of nose and alveolar moulding may influence when surgery should be performed.

Management of Toddlers and Preschool Children with OFC

Conflicts in the feeding, swallowing, and aesthetic processes that OFC youngsters frequently face can result in bad oral health. According to the American Academy of Pediatric Dentistry, this is essential to stress to parents and/or guardians how important it is for all babies, children, and adolescents to build a dental home at this age, especially those who require Special health-care needs. The documenting and communications of caregivers is the first step in creating the dental home, leading to an increased awareness of all concerns that had a significant impacts on the child's oral and dental health.

As early as the first deciduous tooth shows, which typically occurs around age one, it is advisable to launch a dental business. Instead, birth parents ought to be included in a dentist office where comprehensive, progressively approachs a family-oriented, planned, considerate, and culturally successful care is offered and administered or overseen by trained child health specialists. At this time, preventative measures can be used, including fluoride varnish treatment, nutrition counselling, and dental hygiene advice. To ensure appropriate amounts of fluoride in water, the source of the water must also be evaluated (well or municipal water. Fluoride tooth paste can also be used, but only in a small amount, to provide the child with the advantages of fluoride in the prevention of caries with a lesser risk of enamel serious damage to dental fluorosis (a grains of rice sized smears till the child is three year old). To lessen the likelihood of getting dental caries, sugar-based foods must be consumed less frequently and frequently. It is recommended to limit consumption of sugary milk, including chocolate, milk, sodas, and juices, to no more than four per day till the age of six. Children should ideally drink these beverages together with their lunch and dinner and then get their teeth cleaned later. In conclusion, dentists will continues to work with methods for preventing dental caries, giving medical and restorative care as necessary, growth and development monitoring, diet counselling, perioperative care, infant orthopaedics when necessary, and stopping dental caries..

Tooth Development in the Cleft Region

According to studies, patients with OFC have a higher prevalence of dental abnormalities, which have been mostly localised to the region of the cleft defect. These abnormalities include alterations in tooth number and placement as well as smaller teeth. Additionally, children with OFC had a higher incidence of enamel discoloration compared to a regular reference group. This abnormality has primarily been linked to damage during cleft surgery. Hypodontia of the permanent lateral incisor on the cleft side (49.8%) and late root growth in contrast to the contralateral tooth are frequent problems observed in OFC participants. Dental professionals should therefore talk to the parents and guardian about the potential consequences of tooth loss and also the orthodontics and prosthetic solutions available for long-term restoration. In addition to the proactively counselling and preventive care offered at the preschool level, paediatric dentists will give surgical and restorative cares as necessary for OFC kids. Children who have clefs are significantly more likely to have caries affecting their main incisors. A group of kids with OFC had a higher rate of tooth decay in their deciduous dentition than kids without OFC, according to research. Evaluation of children having mixed dentition is necessary to determine the optimal strategy for upcoming alveolar bone grafting.

Patients with CL and CP have a bone deficiency in the alveolar region of the palates, and this is where the teeth are located. Secondly osseous grafting is accepted as an alternative to fill this bone deficiency by providing appropriate alveoli and bony support for the canines to emerge. In patients with OFC, the model time for doing alveolar bone grafting varies according on the individual. However, grafting is incredibly effective in people between the ages of 9 and 12 and when the canines root is developed by roughly a quarter to a half, or before the canine eruption. After surgery, the majority of cleft-area canines will exhibit normal root development and spontaneous eruption thanks to autogenous bone grafting. It is also feasible to expect that the canines might emerge from the bone transplant more progressively, and in a few cases, the eruption process will require surgically and/or orthodontic interventions (exposed and bonded). Due to the pre-separation maxilla's from the upper jaw process, which can be deformed or disconnected from one another, subjects with bi - lateral cleft palate and palate have projecting of the pre-maxilla that advances in countless degrees. The alveolar thickness and height of the teeth next to the cleft deformity may be insufficient, limiting the benefits of orthodontic therapy. During in the stage of mixed dentition, the teeth next to the cleft frequently exhibit good periodontal support despite these development insufficiencies and concerns.

Prior to an alveolar bone graft in these situations, it is better to ignore or properly direct buccal and mesio-distal orthodontic movements as well as rotating motion of the maxillary teeth. Speech is produced in reaction to a significant problem. When surgical treatment is no longer an issue or needs to be postponed owing to a medical issue or the guardian's decision, appliances can be made to assist with speech. Although surgeries is the most popular choice for improving pharyngeal function, certain patients may be candidates for a prosthetic device as an alternative. Like an orthodontic retainer, these particular devices are made to be inserted inside the mouth. For children and various age groups, speech aids are essentially of two types. specifically the speech bulb and the palatal lift. The communicating bulb can be manufactured to partially seal the opening between the soft part of palate and the pharynx in patients with narrow palates. When there is insufficient palate muscle activation, even with sufficient palatal length, the palatal lifting device helps shift the soft part of palate to a spot that makes palatal closure feasible. It is advised that prosthetic devices be created for patients who are at least 5 years old, and that parents or guardians should carefully supervise the use of these devices. Subjects with sub mucous cleft palates (SMCPs) recurrently grieve from overdue diagnosis that can end in compromised speech consequences. Treatment choices may also be complicated by the clinical potential for variation in SMCP severity. Studies have shown that the Magnetic Resonance Imaging (MRI) method is reliable means to detect changes in the location of the velo-pharyngeal muscle. There is information that could be useful in making management and treatment decision. When an alveolar bone graft is necessary, the dentist should consult with dentists and oral and maxillofacial surgeons to lay the framework. They should also think about collaborating with speech therapists whenever a speaking appliance is recommended, stick to preventive dental care measures, and entail surgically removing main teeth from the mouth as necessary.

(A) A youngster with a small soft palate who is 8 years old should have a palatal obturator. The family wants to put off the surgical adjustment.

(b) A 7-year-old child should utilise a palate-lifting appliance to help elevate the palate, which will help to close the palate and lessen nasal air leaks.

Management of Adolescents with OFC

Ofc patients face a constant problem in receiving the best care. The surgically and clinical operations carried out during infancy and early childhood are meant to set the stage for the development of healthy speech, the enhancement of facial symmetry, the development of a successful occlusion, and the strengthening of self-respect. There are rumours, though, that all these earlier involvements could limit maxillary growth, which would then lead to malocclusion and jaw abnormalities, which frequently also influence speech and self-esteem. Young adults with OFC must manage their increased levels of anxiety, which are common of their chronic condition, in addition to the developmental stages that are inevitably present at this age. For example, they must assimilate their facial discrepancies into a changing body image, establish friendships despite potential disappointment with their appearance, interact with medical professionals as teenagers rather than youngsters, and manage their vitality For the purpose of bettering their bite and dental alignment, adolescents frequently undergo orthodontic treatment. Additionally, they are able to receive orthodontic care before the orthodontic procedure that will be carried out once the skeleton is correctly built. When a patient has a massive skeleton class III malocclusion and variable levels of antero-posterior, vertically, and horizontal maxillary growth insufficiency, orthognathic surgery is a viable treatment option. Since pubertal growth starts in late adolescence, many of these kids will require orthognathic surgery. Dental professionals and/or dental assistants can prevent tooth cavities and gingival irritation at this time by offering the teenagers' parents or guardians regular maintenance and oral hygiene instruction. Additionally, restorative therapy with composite resins direct restorations may be necessary for cavitated secondary caries or in rare circumstances for cosmetic changes to anterior teeth. While dental prostheses reintegration is planned, the general dentist must refer the patient to an oral maxillofacial surgeon or consulting dental surgeons for the re-grafts of the deformities region and implant placement. Many general dentists will also refer the patient to a collaborative for the last oral restoration.

Management of Adults with OFC

Adult individuals who've already untreated OFC and require dental care still exist. Unfortunately, the majority of those people either had large clefts that could not be entirely closed with surgery or they were not given the chance to simply have their clefts surgically fixed, leave them with persisting oro-nasal fistulas. The bulk of them will be adolescents or elderly since there was no surgical alternatives for repairs while they were young or perhaps because they did not have appropriate access to good therapy when they were youngsters. Additionally, they could have malformed teeth, extra teeth, or even absent permanent teeth in the area of the cleft. Even after the initial cleft defect has been corrected, some children still develop oro-nasal fistulas and oral clefts (bones discontinuities defects in the alveolus) when they enter adolescence or adulthood. The severity of the remaining defects of the repaired cleft lip and nose may raise additional issues regarding function (particularly communication) and appearance. Concerns about anterior-lateral cross bite, midface hypoplasia, antero-posterior, vertical, and transverse deficiency of the maxilla, upper lip and nasal abnormalities, as well as speech issues, are common in teenagers and young adults who have had cleft defect therapy. End stage restoration might also be best planned for when these carers have attained physiological maturities, which really is normally at age 15 for females and age 16 to 18 or older for males. This is because orthognathic surgical procedure (corrective jaw surgery) can significantly affect face development and growth in patient populations with cleft lip and palate. The maxilla would develop more slowly as well as the mandible would continue to grow if the surgical procedure is carried out before the beginning of facial growth, which could result in the return of the facial deformity and malocclusion. In certain cases, younger surgery may be preferred for aesthetically and psychological reasons, with the knowing that it could need to be repeated once growth is complete.

Prosthetic Reconstruction

Clinicians can be inspired by adult patients who did not receive adequate treatment for cleft palate in terms of prosthesis restoration. Additionally, as individuals become edentulous in later stages of adulthood, prosthetic reconstruction becomes much more complicated. The soft tissue support needed for prosthesis rehabilitation must be sufficient. This component is especially crucial when the relationships between various anatomical parts are carefully taken into account during reconstructive surgery. Patients who can not even receive the appropriate treatment for OFCA frequently have a number of conditions, such as a preterm and collapsed maxillary arch, difficulty breathing, high nasal speech, impaired chewing capacity, hard palate scared tissue, resorbed alveolar bones and ridges, failure of vestibular depths, and oro-nasal fistulas. As patients age and become edentulous, leads to conflict related to OFC accumulation in the body and become confusing in terms of prosthetic restoration. Missing teeth are commonly associated with alveolar clefts. After grafting, the cleft is treated either by allowing the canine to emerge in place of the lost teeth or replacement the tooth with a prosthetic. A natural tooth dental implant, a dental restorations prosthetic (FDP), or a detachable prosthesis are examples of prosthetic techniques. The straightforward goals of prosthodontic therapy include maintaining the remaining teeth and tissue and offering a comfortable, aesthetically pleasing prosthesis that recovers the function of communication, deglutition, mastication, and occlusion.

Palatal Obturator

Even after the cleft has been surgically closed, a residual oro-nasal connection (fistula) may occasionally still exist. Speaking anomalies including unintended nose air output or poor articulation can come from this, which can occur mostly on palate, in the alveolar process of bone, or just in the labial vestibule. The primary objective of a palatal obturator is to seal the gap in order to regain speech. It often changes compensatory articulations and lowers hypernasality. The palate (palatal plate) can be covered by the obturator, which is made of resin acrylic and provides retention using specially made clasps. When surgically correction is not an option, it can be used as could be used as a temporary appliance, and in some older individuals, it can be used as a short term final prosthodontically approaching dental appliance. Although dental restorations prosthesis (FDPs) have a strong historical foundation, they nonetheless present a number of limitations for treating OFC patients. In the tiny FDP group (n=18), there were very few patients with failing teeth, however complications occurred at a rate of 22% throughout the duration of the prolonged observation period (7.4 to 24.9 years).

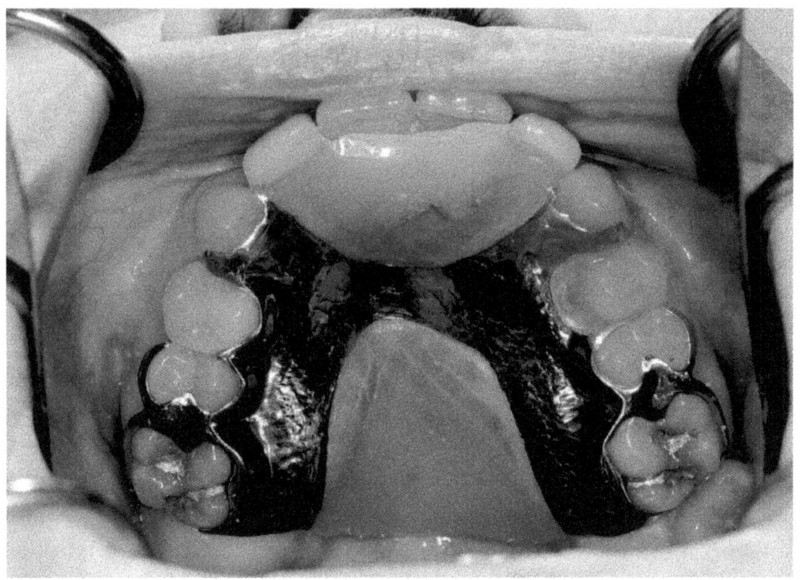

Figure 81: Partial removable prosthesis with palatal obturator repairing not only the cleft palate as well as missing teeth, resulting in functional and esthetic rehabilitation

According to the authors, standard FDP therapy is still the preferred course of treatment even though the contemporary environment makes implant placement challenging. But the limitations on aesthetic and the outcomes as indicated by patients lacked precise definition. The 10-year survival rates of 3 units of FDPs and dental implants were comparable. An FDP must be more complex and have more teeth when used on an OFC patient. Complex FDPs face much greater challenges and do not enjoy the same high percentages of survival. The attaching of removable prosthetics or the removal of neighbouring teeth to make way for a permanently dental prosthesis (FDP) are not permitted during endodontic dental implant therapy. A one dental implant can potentially avoid the higher risks brought on by larger FDPs by stopping the loss of all neighbouring tooth in FDPs. Additionally, and that the use of FDPS without accompanying alveolus regrafting is technically feasible, it nevertheless falls short structurally in addressing the tissue shortage that underlies the lip, alar, and overall face architecture. In individuals with OFC, dental implants have been used as an alternative to traditional tooth replacement methods, although no comprehensive evaluations of this treatment have been published. In observational studies for dental clinical outcomes with OFC, less than 50 subjects have typically been enrolled, and these studies have often only investigated implants survival in general criteria, including patient 's age, gender, as well as types of clefts.

Future Directions

Thanks to developments in cutting-edge technologies for the initial identification of craniofacial anomalies, families may be made aware of the oro-facial clefts before delivery. The advancement of genetic genetics research and the study of families all over the world have allowed for the documentation of the causative genes for a number of syndromes and disorders involving OFCs. Whereas high-resolution 2D imaging is still the cornerstone of prenatal testing, new 3D techniques are further enhancing our ability to accurately detect the facial complexity and cleft defect throughout pregnancy. Early diagnosis permits care of oral and facial cleft defect, the methods to be followed, and any costs connected with therapy till adulthood to be appropriately communicated to families, relatives, guardians, and their friends. Parents can also interact with the other family whose children have oro-facial clefts in order to create a support network and information. The commercialization of a variety of practical adjunctive techniques based on tissue engineering will enhance the results of soft surgical procedures, including the augmentation of bones and the development of new muscles to improve palate function. Innovative cleft repair techniques that involve stem cells may someday replace traditional treatments. The most crucial part of managing kids who really are born with oro-facial malformations is offering comprehensive care that may be efficiently delivered by craniofacial teams.

Clefts and maxillofacial teams are commonly thought of as an active strategy to prevent fragmentation and dehumanisation in the delivery of highly specialised healthcare.

MEDICAL MANAGEMENT:

To avoid neural tube abnormalities, a daily supplementation dose of 0.4 mg of folic acid is currently advised. This is double the daily intake of 0.2 mg for women. It has been proposed that maternal folate supplementation could prevent non-syndromic with oral-facial cleft defect, such as cleft lips even without cleft palate. Folic acid consumption is associated with lower rates of cleft lips and defect of cleft palate, according to numerous academic studies. Some of the problems raised by such earlier studies may be answered by a recent study that showed that the only approach to lower the prevalence of oral cleft defects is by taking higher amounts of folic acid all through the growth of the lips and palate.

Additionally, it has been shown that taking a maternal multivitamin reduces the likelihood of developing cleft lip and significantly lowers the prevalence of cleft palate.

PSYCHOLOGICAL MANAGEMENT

Even if it occurs before birth, the psychological treatment of the cleft subject begins at the moment of diagnosis. A thorough study is essential to the counselling process for the affected families. The referral organisation is concerned with providing the most accurate description of the structural defect that is imaginable. The family feels relieved to think of using orthodontic wire. The design in the majority of these cases will resemble an orthodontic retainer. The prosthodontic obturator could be made using the same guidelines as for the development of detachable partial prostheses, together along with a titanium or Co-Cr alloys metal framework, in adult patients for whom surgically correction is no longer a viable option. Removable prostheses are occasionally advised whenever clefts are not surgically repaired, for the closing of oro-nasal fistulas, but when a speech prosthesis is used to speak to the child and discuss feed, particularly breastfeeding. Parents must talk about the preventive and therapeutic protocols at their own pace, convenience level, and convenience in particular to prepare for the future and to allow them to participate and absorb the information. Inadequate cleft repair may jeopardise social and familial bonds, and the injured child may suffer psychological effects that last a lifetime.

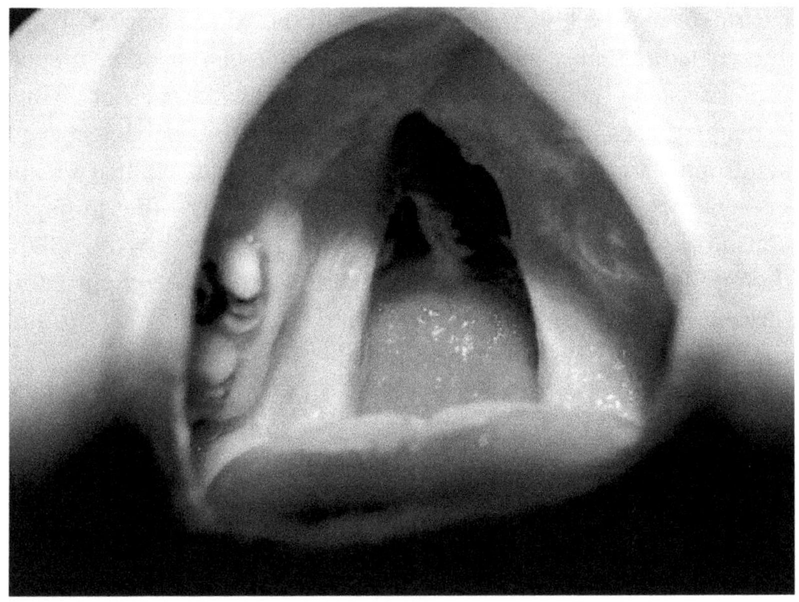

Figure 82: Patient with unrepaired V-shaped cleft of the hard and soft palate.

When a child mature and must deal with the difficulty of individuating with their family and society, psychological counselling may be necessary. There is an opportunity for additional psychological treatments through this whole stage of life because adulthood has its own unique issues for the individual. Parents and guardians want encouragement, comfort, and time to comprehend the information before they can provide the child the care and support they want.

SOCIAL MANAGEMENT

It is important for parents to talk to their children about coping skills for the difficult social situations that arise because of their very own cleft lip and/or birth defect. Strong parental and guardian support systems may stop the growth of a negative self in individuals with cleft palate. For additional management teams like hearing testing, talk therapies, and dento-facial development and treatment may be given, the efficiency of the bodies natural organs and structures must be verified by a psychologist or other mental professional. The craniofacial team is always present while managing cases of cleft palate. An array of craniofacial defects and syndromes are diagnosed and treated by a multidisciplinary team known as a craniofacial team. Additionally, they offer in-depth consultations. The way the topic was handled by the OFCs definitely shows cooperation. This team is strongly committed to making sure that persons with conditions get the aid, attention, and support they require to live better quality lives.

SURGICAL TREATMENTS FOR CLEFT LIP AND CLEFT PALATE DEFECTS:

In order to reduce the irregularity and enable patients to lead normal lives, cleft lips and cleft palate defects care aims to surgically fix the clefts and whatever problems it may bring about. Surgery is used to change the appearance of the face in this treatment. a vocal system that makes speech understandable and teeth that are both functionally ideal and aesthetically pleasing.

Timing of Surgical Repair

One of the most contentious issues between the grouping of surgeon, speech therapist, pathologist, audiologist, and also orthodontist has been and still is the timing of the surgical repair. Without a doubt, the cleft lips is fixed as quickly as possible. Surgeons typically use the well-known "rule of 10" when a newborn is medically appropriate for surgery despite being largely healthy (i.e., 10 weeks of ages, 10 1b in body contain weights, and at very least 10g of haemoglobin in per decilitre of blood collections). Surgery to fix the cleft is delayed even though it is an elective procedure until there are no significant risks to the infant's health from any other medical condition. Unfortunately, there are a number of potential drawbacks for the individual life that could offset any potential advantage of sealing a palatal gap early in childhood. (1) Pharyngeal muscle growth after palatal abnormalities have been corrected is one of the six benefits of early closure.

(2) Ease of feeding, (3) Better phonation skill development

Better oral and nose cleanliness, improved auditory tube function, and improved mental health for both parents and the baby are all benefits.

There are a lot of disadvantages to correcting palatal clefts early in development. The two most important ones are:

(1) Surgery-related scarring impacts maxillary growth restriction; and

(2) Surgical correction is also difficult in younger children with small structures.

Cooperation is a generally recognised value, despite the fact that different cleft teams arrange the surgical repair differently. Depending on various of factors, the soft palatal cleft is fixed between the ages of 8 and 18 months. As soon as medically feasible, the lip is changed. Since it has the positive effects of "shaping" the malformed alveolus, covering the lip as early as feasible is desirable. Similar to how it facilitates eating, it has positive psychological effects on children. After that, the palatal cleft is closed, resulting in the creation of a functional velo-pharyngeal mechanism prior to or concomitant with speech development. Hard palatal clefts are rarely left unrepaired after the repair of the soft palate, especially if they are wide. For as long as it is physically possible, the hard part of the palate clefts is kept open in cases like this to stop the maxillary growing from proceeding freely.

The closing of a hard part of the palatal cleft can be delayed until all of the primary teeth has formed and erupted.

The main issue with evaluating treatment methods is that the final outcomes of surgically repairing clefts can only be manipulated convincingly once the person's growth is initiated. It is disappointing that patients with cleft abnormalities may have treatments that are ultimately disregarded, while follow-up assessments and research indicate inadequate or subpar outcomes, because a surgical technique current in use cannot be carefully examined for 10 to 20 years.

CHEILORRHAPHY

Cheilorrhaphy, a term derived from the Greek words chelotilo, which means lip, and rhaphy, which means connection with the aid of a seam or suture, refers to the surgical treatment of the cleft lip deformity. As early as this is medically feasible, it is frequently the initial surgical technique used to address cleft defects. Split upper lip disturbs the massive circum-oral orbicularis oris muscle. Because this muscle cannot function continuously, the developing components of the maxilla can grow incoherently, emphasising the cleft in the alveolus. At birth, the alveolar process on the unaffected side could seem to extend from the mouth. Premaxillas that protrude from the base of the nose due to improper orbicularis oris-controlled sphincteric muscles regulation have cleft lips on both sides and are unsightly. Therefore, the repair of the lip and the restorations of this muscle sphincter are advantageous for the growth of alveolar segments.

Cheilorrhaphy has two goals:

(1) Practical and

(2) Decorative Objectives: To restore the normal function of the upper lip, the cheilorrhaphy should re-establish the functional organisation of the oris musculature. When the lip is brought into function, an aesthetically undesirable depression will emerge if muscle continuity cannot be restored through area of the cleft.

The vermilion tubercle, cupid's bow, and philtrum are all typical anatomical characteristics of the lip, which is why cheilorrhaphy is done in the second place. In addition to being symmetrical, well-shaped, soft, and supple, the lips must also be scar-free. To correct (at least partially) the nasal deformity caused by the cleft lip is an additional aesthetic need.

Despite the surgeon's ability, these ultimate goals are rarely achieved. Obstacles include the distorted status of the structures prior to surgical intervention and the diminished superiority of tissues inside the cleft edges. Numerous surgical procedures fail to sustain the natural appearance during growing yet do so in an instant. But reasonable results are possible with careful surgical procedure selection.

Surgical techniques:

The surgical procedure required must be unique for each cleft. There are countless procedures that can be utilised for cheilorrhaphy, all of which aim to prolong the cleft borders so that they can be closed. In unilateral circumstances, the unaffected sides serves as a guide for lip length and symmetry. The scar's lines of disintegration are an important design element since they help to reduce lip deformity as well as fibrosis and contracture. Scar contracture causes the lips to close in a linear pattern and results in a distinctive notching of the upper lip. If any hope of developing normal function exists, consideration of the re - orientation and union of the lip's musculature is of the utmost importance. Procedures like cheilorrhaphy aid in restoring symmetry to the lip and nasal tip. The cleft deformity and nasal encompassing via the floor of the nose impair the continuousness of both the nose apparatus. A collapsing of the nose occurs when the alar cartilage's bony support is lost. Once the lip has closed, it is imperative to reposition this laterally dislocated tissue toward the midline. Thus, the first and most important step in treating the nasal deformities that so many cleft patients have is cheilorrhaphy.

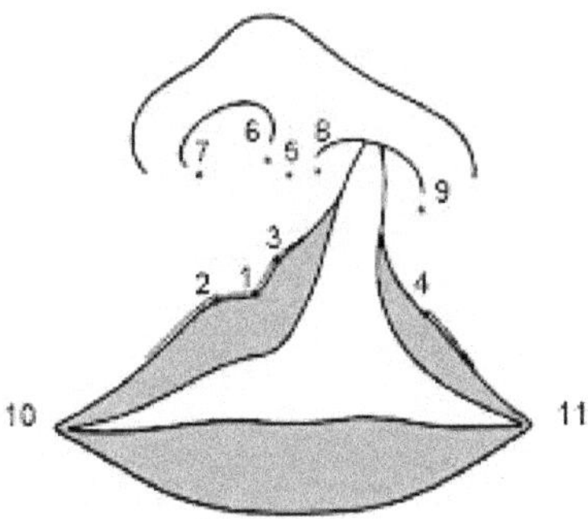

Anatomic Landmarks

Figure 83: The Millard Cheiloharrhaphy technique (anatomicallandmarks)

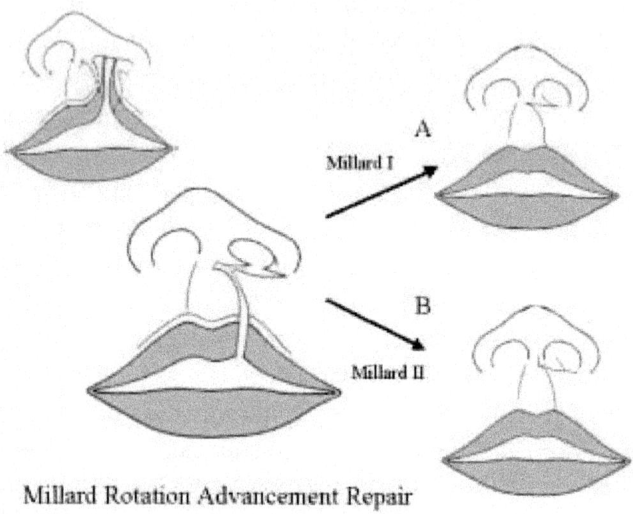

Figure 84: The Millard Cheiloharrhaphy technique

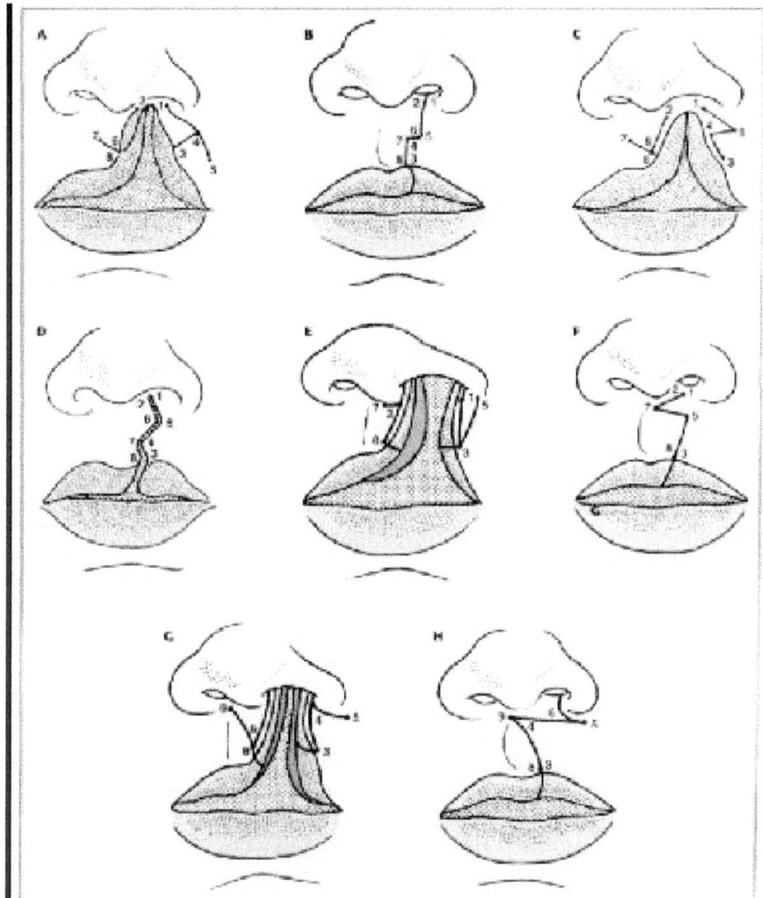

Figure 85: Several Cheilorrhophy techniques. A and B, le. Mesurier technique tor incomplete unilateral cleft. C and D. Tennison operation. E and F, Wynr operation. C and H, Millard operation (i.e.., rotation advancement technique).

Palatorrhaphy

Palatorrhaphy is commonly completed in a single procedure, but rarely requires two. The soft palate closure, or staphylorrhaphy, is typically carried out first in two surgeries, followed by the hard palate closure, or uranorrhaphy.

Objective:

The basic objective of cleft palate repair is to develop a speaking and deglutition-capable mechanisms without materially obstructing future maxillary growth. Therefore, attaining these objectives requires establishing a robust velo-pharyngeal system and dividing the oral and nasal chambers.

Excessive removing of soft tissue from bone can cause scarring, which will have a detrimental effect on maxillary growth. The goal is to generate a soft part of the palate that really is long, mobile, and able to produce regular speech. The combination of the surgeries taken into consideration and the age at which they have been established are specified by the problem's risky nature.

Surgical techniques:

Every cleft on the palate is distinct. They differ in terms of palatal length, comprehensiveness, width, and how much exposing hard and soft tissue there is. As a result, not just from one surgeon to the next but also from one patient to the next, there are many different surgical techniques utilised to close cleft palate abnormalities.

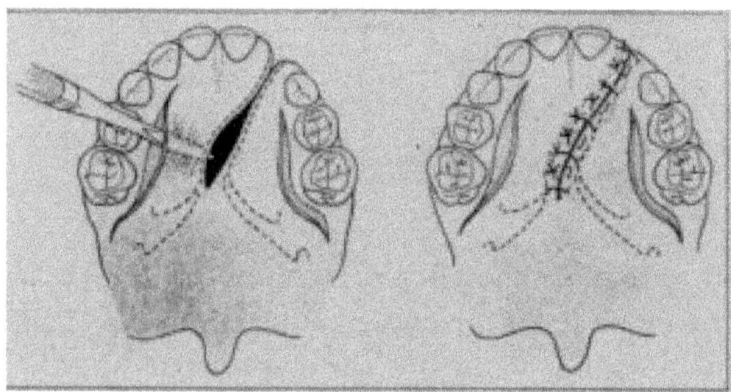

Figure 86: Von Langenbeck operation for closure of hard palate by giving lateral releasing incisions. This technique is one-layer closure-nasal (i.e., superior) aspect of palatal flaps will epithelialize, as will denuded areas of palatal bone

Closure of the hard palate: Only soft tissues are used to close the hard palate. Creating an osseous barrier between the nasal and oral canals is typically not attempted. The quality of the soft tissues varies along the cleft border. Some are primarily useless and atrophic in nature. They appear healthy elsewhere and give themselves voluntarily to dissection and suture uprightness. When it is possible to estimate the size of the cleft defect, the soft tissues are separated from of the palatal shelves and slit all along cleft margin. Regular lateral relaxing incisions next to the teeth are needed for this procedure. Thus, the soft tissues are sutured over the cleft defect in a watertight manner and allowed to recover. The portions of bone exposed by the laterally relaxing incisions are permitted to heal as a secondary goal. The superior section of the palate flaps also undergoes re-epithelialization together with the respiratory epithelium because this area is presently the nasal floor lining. Two different layer closing of the hard part of the palatal cleft defect is ideal whenever it is possible. To do this, the nasal mucosa from of the septum, lateral wall, and floor of the nose must be organised and stitched together prior to the oral closure. When the mucosa is lengthy and connected towards the palatal shelf immediately across from cleft defects, it is lifted from in the vomer bone and sewn to the palate tissues on the affected cleft side.

The vomer flap procedure requires a small amount of palatal muco-periosteum removal and produces little scar contraction.

Vomer's exposed areas and the flap's opposite sides, which are epithelium-free, frequently become epithelized. When the vomer is readily available for usage and the cleft is not too large, the vomer flap procedure is useful since it creates a one-layer closure.

The most difficult procedure performed on a cleft patient is the closure of the soft palate, according to government statistics. Accessibility is the main problem since the soft part of the palate is situated to reaching the backside of the oral mucosa. Light retraction problems are complicated by the fact that the doctor can only operate from the oral sides while having to address the soft part of the palate on both the nasal and oral sides. The medical professional might also have to work with exceedingly thin, atrophic tissues while still creating a closure that will help it keep together even healing is still occurring. To aid in achieving this, the soft palate always is closed in three layers, always in the same order: nasal mucosa, muscle, and oral mucosa.

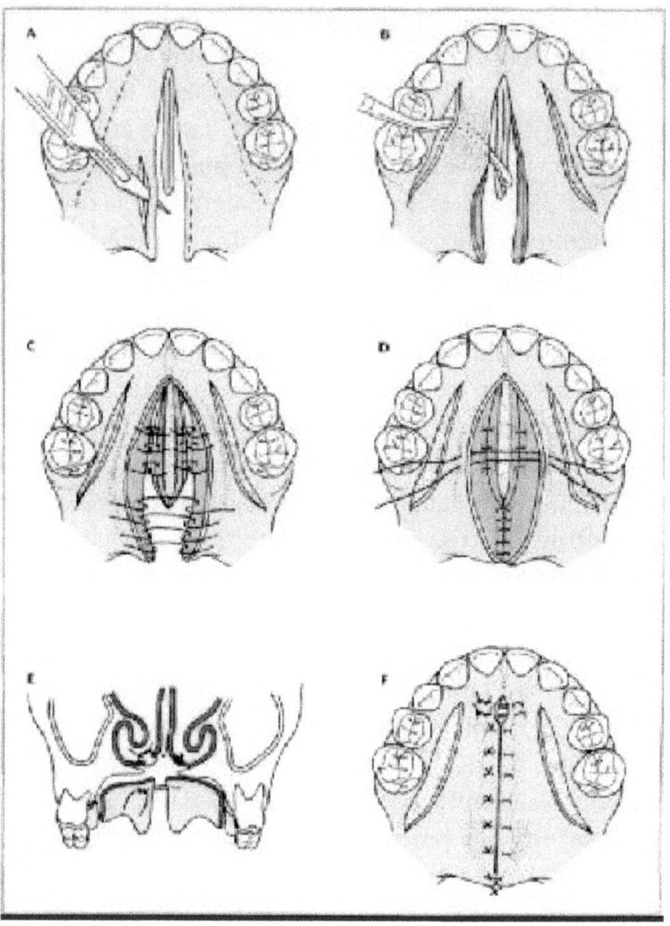

Figure 87: Variation of von Langenbeck operation for concomitant hard and soft palate closure. It three-layer closure for soft palate (i.e., nasal mucosa, muscle, oral mucosa) and two-

layer closurefor hard palate (i.e., flapi from vomer and nasal door to produce nasal closure, palatal flaps for oral closure). A, Removing mucosa from margin of cleft. B, Mucoperiosteal flaps on hard palate are developed;note lateral releasing incisions. C, Sutures placed into nasal mucosa alter development of nasal flaps from vomer and nasal floor. Sutures are placed that knots will be on nasal side. D, Nasal mucosa has been closed. E, Frontal section showing repair of nasal mucosa. nasal F, Closure of oral mucoperiosteum,

The edges of the cleft are cut at the posterior end of the hard palate and, at most, at the distal end of the uvula (some surgeons transfer the incision and closure down to the palate-pharyngeal fold in order to extend the soft palate). After being separated from the underlying muscles, the nasal mucosa is sutured to the mucosa on the opposite end. The muscular layer needs to be handled with exceptional and specific care. The muscle of the soft palate is exhibited posterior aspect and laterally along the borders of the hard palate by being decided to bring across to the opposite side. Muscle attachments need to be released from their bone insertions and repositioned so that they are roughly in line with the other ends. The velo-pharyngeal mechanism has a chance to function properly only then. If there isn't enough muscular tissue to properly examine that musculature in the midline, the pterygoid hamuluar structures can be broken, release the tensor palatini muscle nearby. Especially with severe clefts, this treatment is usually required. Rarely is it discovered also that soft part of the palate is small and that it is difficult for it to articulate with the pharyngeal wall. Particularly with partial palatal clefts that just impact the soft palate, this situation is more frequent.

In these circumstances, the palate may be addressed in a manner that lengthens it as well as unites the two lateral portions toward the midline. A so W-Y push-back method (Wardill) and U- type of shaped rollback procedure are commonly preferred (Dorrance and Brawn). The hard palate's muco-periosteum is sliced and raised in such a way that it enables both the hard and soft palate's soft tissue rudiments to extend posteriorly, resulting in palatal length. Neither the special surgical procedure for cleft lips nor cleft palate normally corrects the alveolar cleft abnormality. As a result, the affected person may still have an oro-nasal fistula in this area, and the cleft defect will prevent the maxillary alveolus from growing continuously.

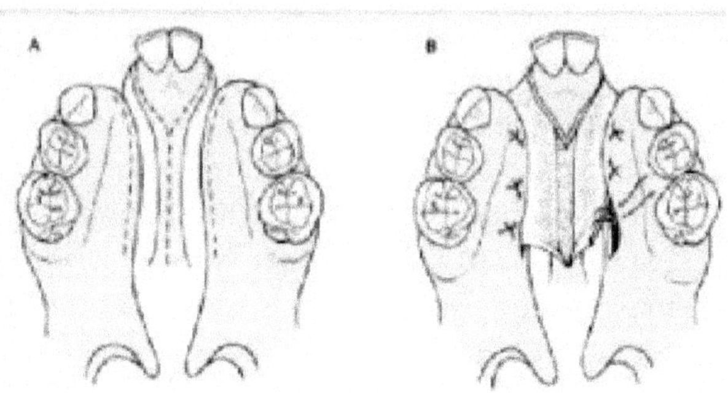

Figure 88: Vomer flap technique for closure of hard palate cleft (bilateral in this case). A, Incisions through nasal mucosa on underside of nasal septum (i.e., vomer) and mucosa of cleft margins. B, Mucosa of nasal septum is dissected off nasal septum and inserted under palatal mucosa at margins Of cleft. This is one-layer nasal closure only. Connective tissue undersurface of nasal mucosa will epithelialize.

Five issues could arise just as a result of this:

Nasal secretions drain through into oral cavity, teeth emerge into alveolar gap, the alveolar segments collapse, oral secretions leak into nasal cavity, the alveolar segments collapse, and, if a cleft is large in size, speech is badly damaged.

Bone grafts for alveolar clefts can offer a number of advantages.

They are primarily useful in assisting in the unification of the alveolar segments and in preventing collapses and constrictions of the alveolar arch, which is crucial in particular cases when the maxilla have undergone orthodontic extension. The second benefit of alveoli cleft bone grafts is that they offer bone supports for teeth that emerge into the clefts as well as teeth that emerge near to the cleft defect. On the distal end of the central incisor, the bone support is typically thin and varies in height. Due to a lack of bone support, these teeth frequently exhibit a modest degree of movement. This tooth's alveolar bone can be combined to protect its periodontal conservation. The canine maintains strong periodontal supports during and after eruption, emerging into the clefts site and well within the healthy bone put into the cleft defect. Alveolar cleft grafts' third benefit is the approximate closure of an oro-nasal fistula, which will separate the nasal and oral chambers and prevent fluid from leaking between them.

The fourth advantage is an extension of the alveolar ridge along the cleft. It creates a more suitable supporting basis, enabling the use of dental prostheses. The sixth benefit just so occurs to be the formation of a solid foundations for the lips and alar bottom of the nose. Even if they lacked a firm osseous foundation prior to the graft, the tissue at the bottom of the nose are strengthened after alveoli cleft grafting, proving that the procedure itself improves the nasal structure. As a result, nose alterations must be finished before the alveolar graft.

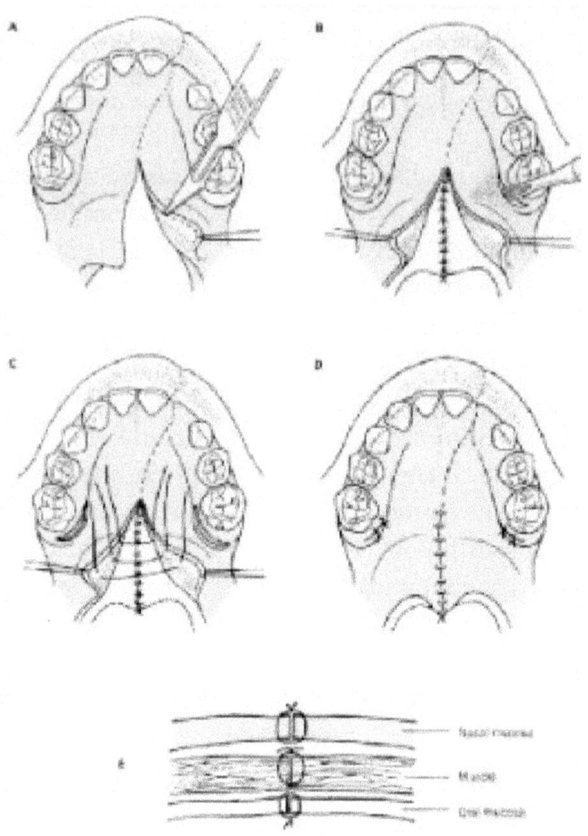

Figure 89 : Triple-layered soft palate closure. A, Excision of mucosa at cleft margin. B, Dissection of nasal mucosa from soft palate to facilitate closure. Nasal mucosa is sutured together with knots tied or nasal (i.e., superior) surface. This maneuver releases tensor veli palatini and facilitates approximation in midline. C, Muscle *h* dissected from insertion into hard palate, and sutures are placed to approximate muscle in midline, D, Closure of oral mucosa is accomplished last. E. Layered closure of soft palate.

Timing of graft procedure:

Alveolar cleft grafting is usually performed on patients between the ages of 7 and 10.By the conclusion of this period, the majority of maxillary growth should have taken place, and the operation to close the alveolar cleft shouldn't negatively impact the maxilla's future growth. The graft must be in situ before the permanent canines emerge into the cleft defect in order to protect the periodontal support. The grafting procedure is best carried out when between 50 and 70 percent of the canine root has formed. It is equally effective to do orthodontic arch expansion before or after the treatment. However, some surgeons choose to enlarge previous to bone grafting so that accessibility into the cleft area is made possible during surgery.

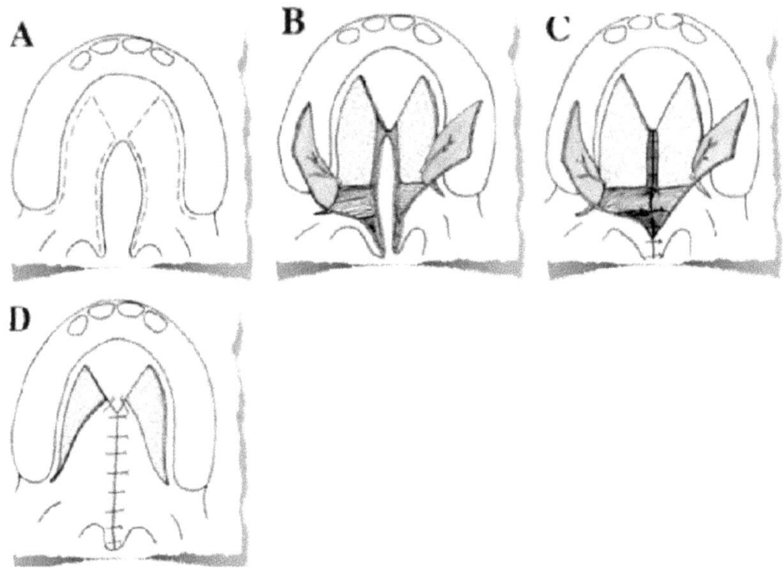

Figure 90 : The Wardill operations for palatal lengthening on closure , A and B, Four-flap operation for extensive cleft. C and D, Three-flap operation for shorter cleft

Surgical procedure:

Bone grafts inserted into the alveolar cleft should be covered by unharmed muco-periosteal flaps on both ends. This indicates that nasal and palatal mucosa as well as labial mucosa flap must all be produced and suturing with in an appropriate tension-free, watertight manner in order to avoid contamination of the graft. These issues exist in every treatment, regardless of how the soft tissues incision for alveolar cleft grafts are done. The alveolar cleft is usually filled with the patient's bone. Allogeneic bone is used by a limited percentage of surgeons, nonetheless (i.e Homologous bone from any another individual). The graft are made into the a particulate stability and filled into the location of the defect after that the nasal and palatal mucosa have been roughly approximated. After that, the labial mucosa is usually located over the bone transplant. These grafts are progressively replaced with new bones that is cloudy and difficult to distinguish from the surrounding alveolar process. While emergence of teeth into the graft sites typically proceeds undisturbed, orthodontic movement of teeth that are approximated around them is theoretically conceivable.

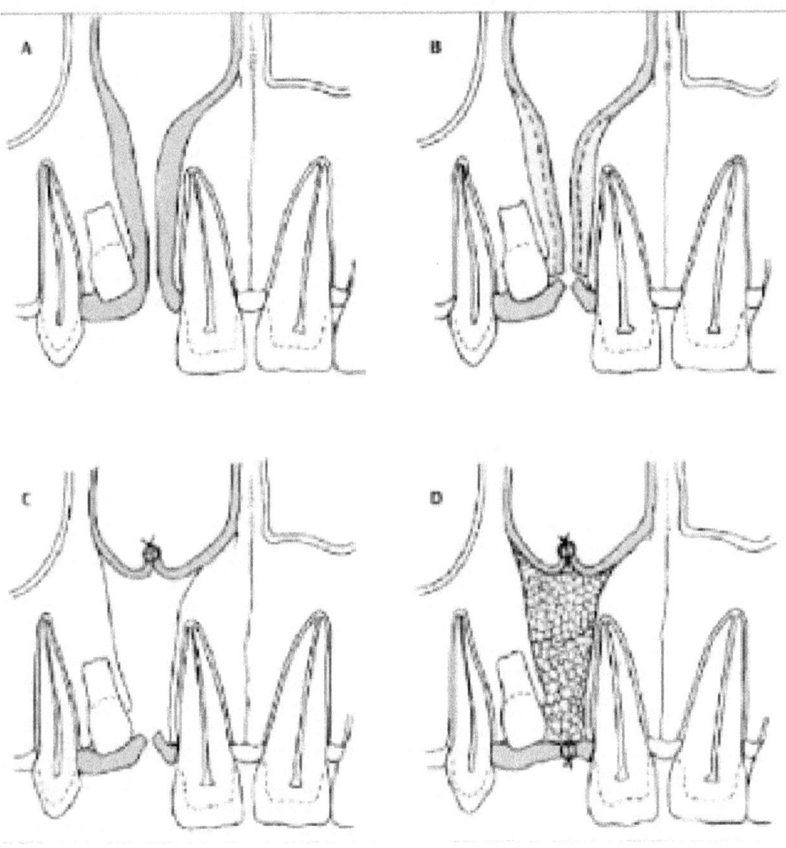

Figure 91: Technique for alveolar cleft bone grafting. A, Preoperative defect viewed from labial aspect. Fistula extends, into nasal cavity. B, Incision divides mucosa fistula, which allows development of nasal and oral flaps. C, Mucosal flap developed from lining of fistula is turned inward, up into nasal cavity, and sutured in watertight manner D, Bone graft material is packed into cleft, and oral mucosa is closed in watertight manner.

Correction of Maxillo- mandibular Disharmonies

The participant with a cleft deformities frequently displays transversal upper jaw constrictions and retrusions as a result of cicatricial contraction from prior surgeries. In many cases, the linked malocclusion precludes orthodontic therapy when it is administered alone. However, due to various abnormalities and scars that are present in the maxilla of cleft patients, there haven't been many changes made to the technical components of maxillary surgery. Overall, complete maxillary osteotomies are necessary for maxilla development and rarely for maxilla widening. Up many instances, the damaged alveolar cleft area's impacted alveolus is moved anteriorly to roughly fill in a portion of the space. These finishing operations need the segment of the upper jaw, which has typically previously been done, due to the shape of the cleft. There are two characteristics that set a person with a cleft apart from subject without a clefts : the scar that spans the palate and the reduced blood supply to the maxilla.

Widening of the maxilla is exceedingly difficult due to scarring from prior surgeries, and it is crucial to repeatedly remove some of the affected tissue. Due to the limited blood supply the cleft maxilla receives, the doctor should try to be careful and maintain as much muco-periosteum as possible in the maxilla. Additionally, caution must be used to avoid creating another oro-nasal fistula. If the alveolar cleft needed to be grafted, it might be done during the same procedure. However, in bilateral clefts, the pro-labial section receives very little blood flow. In such cases, it may be wise to perform the alveoli cleft grafts first, followed by an each maxillary osteotomy once enough time has passed for the circulation of the damaged pro-labial segment. The subject with a cleft palate in the maxilla faces challenges since the progression processes are planned in a way that impacts the velo-pharyngeal mechanism. The soft palate is also dragged forward as a result of the maxilla being carried forward. The postoperative phase may render a subject's preoperative marginal ability of the velo-pharyngeal system ineffective. Controlling which subjects will fall victim to this issue is quite difficult. Though secondary palatal or pharyngeal surgical methods to increase velo-pharyngeal ability are discussed with the concerned person due to the existential probability of this ineffectiveness. These treatments can be completed later, if necessary.

Secondary Surgical Procedures

After the first restoration of cleft defects, further surgical treatments are performed in an effort to enhance speech or correct lingering problems. The pharyngeal flap technique is the most frequently chosen secondary surgical procedure to improve velo-pharyngeal capabilities. In this particular method, the posterior part of pharyngeal wall is elevated, and the superlative side of the soft part of the palate is injected with a broad vertical strips of pharyngeal mucous membranes and musculature. These flaps often have a higher base. Pharyngeal flap's advancement left a hole in the posterior pharyngeal wall, which can be filled in predominantly or still needs to undergo secondary healing. The pharynx and soft palate join once they are inserted into the soft palate, leaving two lateral portions as the aperture between the oropharynx and naso-pharynx. As a result, there is less airflow between the oro- and naso-pharynx. The elevation of the soft palate and constriction of the medial pharyngeal wall are both parts of the velo-pharyngeal mechanism. As a new biocompatible material is situated behind posterior part pharyngeal walls in order to be introduced anteriorly, a previously recognised alternate method has come under further scrutiny. As a result, the soft palate must travel less distance to approach the naso-pharynx. The ultimately make of this approach that have historically been encountered include the displacement of the implant as well as infection, which commonly necessitates removal.

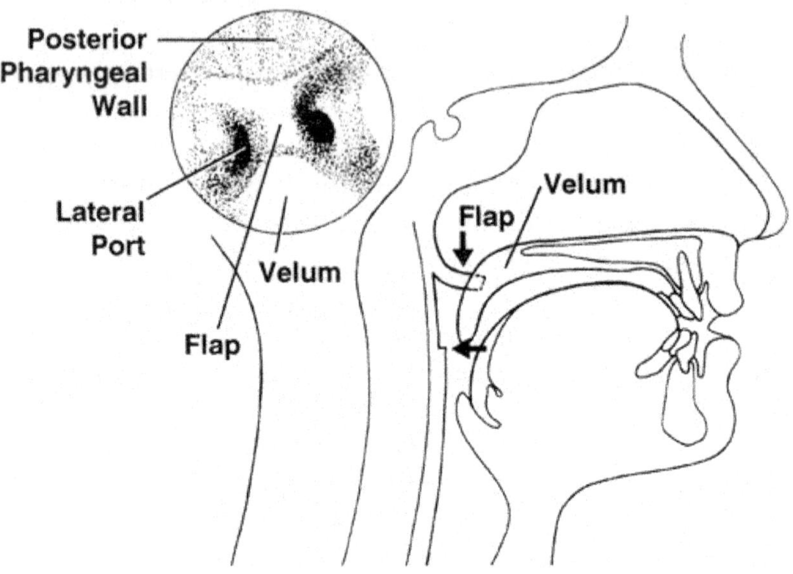

Figure 92: Superiorly based pharyngeal flap. Flap is sutured to superior aspect of soft palate, thus partially partitioning oral and nasal cavities from one another. Only nasal airway remaining after this overation is two lateral openings on each

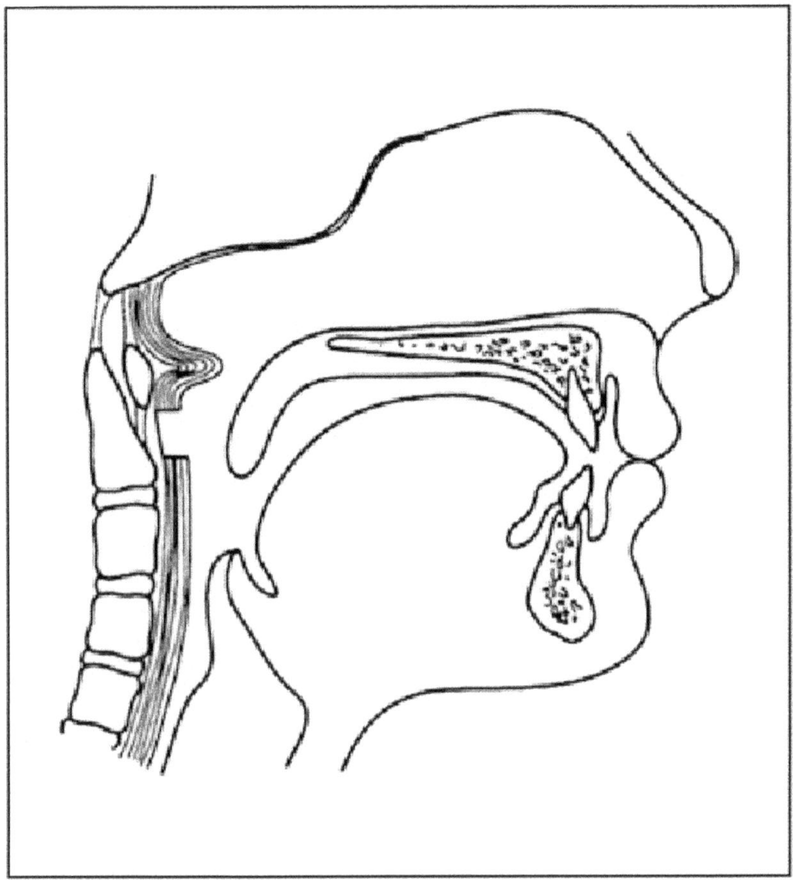

Figure 93 : Posterior pharyngeal wall implant. This makes distance between soft palate and pharyngeal wall smaller so that velopharyngeal closure is facilitated

DENTAL NEEDS HAVE CLEFT AFFLICTED INDIVIDUALS

Dentists will encounter cleft patients in their extensive practise due to the relatively higher proportion of people who are affected. Since these individuals' dental demands do not much differ from those of other beings, they shouldn't encounter any enormous obstacles. However, whether the cleft is fixed or left untreated, these people have a few specific requirements that the dentist should be aware of. Due to the interdisciplinary approach that cleft patients require, the dentist must be mindful of and aware of the full treatment plan put out by the cleft team for the management of the patient. The presenting of any costly or irreversible procedures on tooth that may be scheduled for removal in the near future is prevented by awareness of this method. For instance, using a bridges to restore a congenitally missing lateral incisors before alveolar graft and orthodontic treatment is considered undesirable. Extraction of additional teeth that might be temporarily kept in place to maintain alveolar bone support is also harmful. Till the orthodontic, orthognathic, and alveolar grafting operations are finished, all fixed bridgework should be postponed. Only then will hygienist be able to precisely control the available ridge form and space for pontics. Additionally, the maxillary arch's two halves will move independently until they are joined together with the use of bone grafts, and bridgework crossing the cleft margin may be prone to becoming loose.

Pediatric dentist must be capable of communicating with the other specialists dealing with the patient's numerous cleft issues without difficulty in order to plan services properly. The teeth near to the cleft edges may not only be absent or deformed, and also lacking periodontal support due to their location in the cleft defects margin and absence of bone. Since their teeth are frequently rotated and misaligned, this condition predisposes those to periodontitis and preterm loss if they are not maintained in a margin of optimal health. As a result, oral hygiene procedures may be more difficult for these people, necessitating more frequent prophylactic and superior oral hygiene guidance with careful corroboration. If not, extensive cavity and early loss could happen. Since the cleft patient may have fewer teeth accessible for use in necessary duties, this is a special tragedy for them (Eg: retaining orthodontic, orthopaedic, or speech appliances).

PROSTHETIC SPEECH AID APPLIANCES

Prosthetic maintenance may be necessary for the cleft defect isssue for two reasons: First, since missing teeth are so common in people with cleft palates, they should have replacement teeth. Second, a dentist can create a speech assist for persons who regretfully were unable to achieve velo-pharyngeal competency through surgical adjustments to minimise hyper-nasal speaking. An acrylic bulb linked to a tooth-borne gadget in the maxilla makes up a speech assisting device. The bulb then raises the soft palate superiorly and is roughly positioned to contact its underside. A second acrylic protrusion, known as a bulb obturator, can be placed to extends onto the backside of the palate if the functions of this bulb is insufficient. As a result, the pharyngeal isthmus narrows, and the size can be altered for best results. When this particular bulb is functioning, the posterior pharyngeal wall will come into contact with it. As the pharyngeal musculature gets more active, the size of the bulb may occasionally decrease. Two situations call for this specific kind of appliance

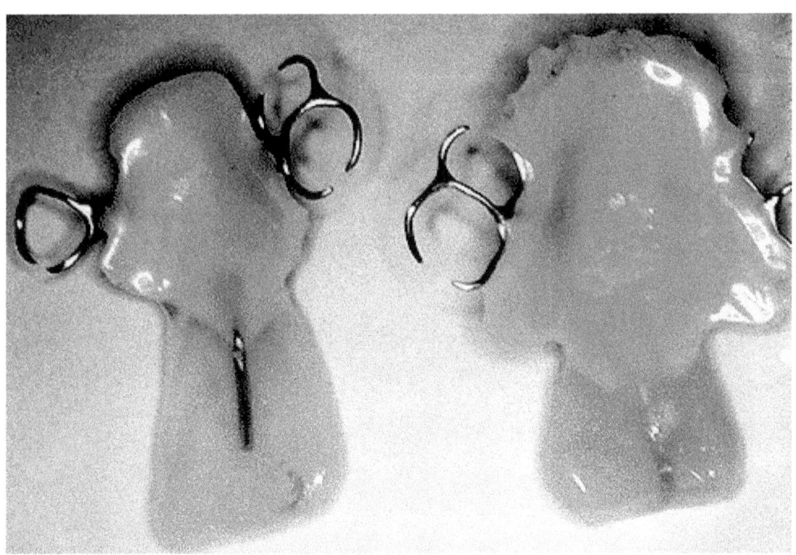

1. **Figure 94: Prosthetic speech aid appliances designed appliances.**
2. **A and B, both to lift soft palate and to obturate oral and nasal cavities**

In order to improve muscle activity prior to pharyngeal flap surgery, or because secondary surgical procedures are ineffective at generating velo-pharyngeal competence. By significantly expanding into the labial sulcus, the speech-improving appliance also helps to sustain underdeveloped upper lips and avoid the need for prosthetic dental replacements. It is obvious that maintaining the residual teeth in the best possible condition is a prerequisite for effective speech aid device therapy.

CHAPTER TWELVE

FUTURE OF CLEFT LIP AND PALATE RESEARCH IN INDIA

Indian consanguinity and clefts

India was recognised as a world leaders in society gene following the census of 187, having one of the earliest documents to show the occurrence of a number of diseases and impairments, including leprosy, blindness, deafness, and insanity. India has made enormous strides in the fight against infectious disease through advancements in sanitation, nutrition, immunizations, and other public health initiatives. As a result, genetic issues are now receiving more attention. Recessive genetic illnesses are one example of how consanguinity affects the wide range of human diseases, yet the effects of consanguineous marriage have purposefully not been listed in relation to numerous diseases. There is very little information available regarding how consanguinity affects cleft lip and palate or other craniofacial defects. In the Northern, Eastern, and North Eastern states, consanguineous marriages are rare, according to the National Family and Health Survey (NFHS) during the years 1992–1993, this is due to the overwhelming Hindu population in these regions. Contrarily, consanguineous marriages between biological relatives are a long-standing tradition in Southern India.

The largest percentages are seen in the states of Andhra Pradesh, Karnataka, and Tamil Nadu; Kerala is an exception because the state's sizable Christian population strictly forbids consanguineous unions.

Research into consanguineous marriage's implications on non-syndroms of cleft lips and palate would seem useful in the promotion of genetic studies into these and other craniofacial and cleft lip and palate disorders. This might be incorporated into the much anticipated INDIANCRAN cleft lips and cleft palate studies that is slated for India. It was debated how to handle the large liability of craniofacial malformations in India following a series of consensus sessions. The WHO provided its support for this. Additionally, those specific Indian delegates expressed a great willingness to take part in and do something to improve quality. These provided the framework for advanced treatment organization, cross-center research projects linking results, planned offices for the gathering of group core outcomes evidence, and involvement in international research projects. Because of the pure duty of earlier generations, a section of the population aged with unresolved clefts has significant surgery and many types of rehabilitative therapy, helping to reduce the vast number of cleft cases in India. To date, however, there have also been relatively little attempts to analyse clinical outcome, compare treatment philosophies between centres, determine whether an impairment still exhibits residual abnormality, or put performance improvement techniques into action.

An approved pilot study was implemented to start the process of establishing baseline cleft care guidelines in country India and to supports the Indian craniofacial At the Indian Society for Cleft Lip and Palate and Craniofacial Anomalies Meeting in Guwahati, Assam, in 2006, WHO presented clinical studies. This project aimed to do is provide preliminary data that was primarily aimed at the high volume of organisations between these outcomes and tries to claim of superior cares and the likelihood of organisations within and without the India. It also aimed to enable treatment programs to take part in WHO volume treatment organisations. The overall goal of this study is to soon improve the level of cleft cares in India. Six cleft lip and palate treatment organisations in India participated on the research entitled "Assessment of treatment success of cleft lip and palate surgery in non-syndromic complete unilateral cleft lip/palate kids at 5years of age." The completion of inter-center and international tests was made possible by the outcome component, and accepted standard and reputable research techniques. The results of this pilot study showed that Indian cleft facilities may participate in international comparisons, and they might be published in a subsequent issue of a Indian Journal of Plastic Surgery. "Indian collaboration on craniofacial anomalies" project, often known as "INDIACRAN," is a research endeavour that aims to tackle the challenges of aetiology and the standard of cleft treatment through a coordinated multi-center strategy. This objectifies to adopt a broad-based multi-disciplinary approach in order to address

(a) Quality of treatment offered by inter-center judgments

(b) Aetiology through a gene-environment communication addressal.

On September 2, 2007, a discussion titled "Addressing the Challenge of Birth Defects and Craniofacial Anomalies in India" was conducted at the Asian Pacific Cleft Palate Congress in Goa under the auspices of a WHO Collaborating Center.

Using this media, the Indian Council of Medical Research (ICMR) determined the current efforts and priorities in human genetics research in India.

One of the objectives of a Indian National Task Force on Human Genetics is the development of a comprehensive database on genetic anomalies, including birth defects. With the aid of a country-wide network of genetic centres that can offer clinicals to construct antenatal diagnosis, integrated and lab diagnosis, counselling, and molecular methods, a national database on genetic disorders, include birth defects, can be established. To expand the number of professionals with the necessary training in a variety of occupations, including medical consultant, scientist, information technicians, laboratories technologist, counsellor, and social worker, The description of new disease genes that are exclusive to India such as Handigodu disease, calcific pancreatic inflammation, hypertrophic cardiomyopathy, etc., may also contain genetic predisposition to cancer and complex polygenic illnesses. A thorough analysis of the relationship between genotype and phenotype as well as gene-gene and gene environment communications are being done in numerous genetically identifiable assemblies in India in order to understand the variability of illnesses.

CHAPTER THIRTEEN

CONCLUSION

For the proper management of a child with CLCP, a thorough understanding and accurate diagnosis of the orofacial cleft and any related disorders are essential. Second, a multidisciplinary mind set is necessary for such issues. Finally, parental counselling is crucial before beginning any type of treatment since it can be quite difficult for parents to acknowledge the subject's illness and because doing so causes them a lot of psychological stress. When these challenges are overcome, we get a better response and recognition from the subject's feeding habit. For the evaluation of the issues and hazards experienced by the child subject, recognition of the linked malformations and disorders with the mouth cleft is crucial. It is crucial to have a good understanding of the deformities associated to orofacial clefts in order to give the appropriate care to improves the survivability of these affected children. With the aid of NGOs, India's outdated unmet needs in terms of initial cleft repair are progressively being addressed, and there seems to be no scarcity of clinical knowledge. WHO has supported the ideas of a multidisciplinary approach to therapy, and the Indian craniofacial community has acknowledged these ideas. Although several craniofacial organisations in country India were taking a multidisciplinary approaching to the management and there were currently few professionals who are proficient in both psychology and speech and language therapy. Orofacial clefts and other craniofacial defects are not uncommon in India, but accurate statistics on their incidence are not yet available because birth defect reporting and ascertainment continue to provide significant challenges. There is agreement to improve birth defects research and investigations in order to identify the prevalence of orofacial deformities at birth, improving care and determining the genetic and environmental causes of cleft defects in country India.

The "Indiacran" research project, a multi-center attempt organised by WHO collaboration organisations, is presently has been used to explain the different features of the Indian subcontinent's community that influence research through both therapy and aetiology.

CHAPTER FOURTEEN

REFERENCE

1. Orofacial Clefts: A Worldwide Review of the Problem Volume 2013 (2013) Article ID 348465, P. Agbenorku

2. G. L. Wehby and J. C. Muray, "Folic acid and orofacial clefts: a review of the evidence. Oral Diseases, vol. 16, no. 1, pp. 11-19, 2010. View at Publisher

3. P. Mossey and J. Little, "Addressing the challenges of cleft lip and palate

research in India," Indian Journal of Plastic Surgery, vol. 42. no. 1. pp. S9-S18,

2009

4. Cleft Lip and Palate,http://en.wikipedia.org/wiki/Cleft_lip_and_palate

5. B. J. Leonard and J. D. Brust, "Self-concept of children and adolescents with

cleft lip and/or palate," Cleft Palate-Craniofacial Journal, vol. 28, no. 4, pp. 347-

353, 1991.

6. E. Ellis III, "Management of patients with orofacial clefts," in Contemporary

Oral and Maxillofacial Surgery, pp. 623-645, Mosby, St. Louis, Mo, USA. 4th

edition, 2003.

7. F. Blanco-Davila, "Incidence of cleft lip and palate in the northeast of Mexico: a 10-year study," The Journal of Craniofacial

Surgery, vol. 14, no. 4., pp. 533-537, 2003.

8. T. D. Gregg, D. Boyd, and A. Richardson, "The incidence of cleft lip and palate in Northern Ireland from 1980-1990," British Journal of Orthodontics, vol. 21, no. 4, pp. 387-392, 1994.

9. T. Hartridge, H. M. Illing, and J. R. Sandy, "The role of folic acid in oral clefting" British Journal of Orthodontics, vol. 26, no. 2. pp. 115-120, 1999.

10. K. J. Rothman, L. L. Moore, M. R. Singer, U. S. D. T. Nguyen, S. Mannino, and A. Milunsky, "Teratogenicity o high vitamin A intake." The New England Journal of Medicine, vol. 333, no. 21, pp. 1369-1373, 1995.

11. White Memorial Medical Center (Adventist Health) Cleft Palate Program, http://www.whitememorial.com/medicalservices/cleft-palate-faqs.

12. J. C. Murray and B. C. Schutte, "Cleft palate: players, pathways, and pursuits," The Journal of Clinical Investigation, vol. 113, no. 12, pp. 1676-1678, 2004.

13. L. Scapoli, J. Marchesini, M. Martinelli et al., "Investigation of the W 185 X

nonsense mutation of PVRLI gene in Italian nonsyndromic cleft lip and palate

patients," American Journal of Medical Genetics, vol. 127, no. 2, p. 211, 2004.

14. Sperber, GH. Formation of the primary palate. In: Wyszynski, DF., editor. Cleft Lip and Palate: From Origin to Treatment. Oxford University Press; 2002. p. 5- 13.

15. Rahimov F, Marazita ML, Visel A, Cooper ME, Hitchler MJ, Rubini M,

Domann FE, Govil M, Christensen K, Bille C, Melbye M, Jugessur A, Lie RT,

Wilcox AJ, Fitzpatrick DR, Green ED, Mossey PA, Little J, Steegers Theunissen RP. Pennacchio LA, Schutte BC, Murray JC. Disruptionof an AP 2alpha binding site in an IRF6 enhancer is associated with cleft lip. Nat Genet. 2008; 40:1341-7 [PubMed: 18836445]

16. EE, Machida J, Natsume N, Murray JC. Complete sequencing shows a role for MSXI in non-syndromic cleft lip and palate. J Med Genet. 2003: 40:399-407. [PubMed: 12807959]

17. Lidral AC, Moreno LM. Progress toward disceming the genetics of cleft lip. Curr Opin Pediatr. 2005 Dec; 17(6):731-9. Review. [PubMed: 16282779).

18. Shi M, Christensen K, Weinberg CR, Romitti P, Bathum L, Lozada A, Moris RW, Lovett M, Murray JC. Orofacial cleft risk is increased with maternal smoking and specific detoxification-gene variants. Am J Hum Genet. 2007 Jar 80(1):76-90. [PubMed: 17160896]

19. Fedik Rahimov, Astanand Jugessur, Jeffrey C. Murray, M.D. Genetics of

Nonsyndromic Orofacial Clefts. Cleft Palate Craniofac J. 2012 Jan; 49(1): 73-91.

20. Lammer EJ, Shaw GM, lovannisci DM, Finneli RH. Maternal smoking. Genetic variation of glutathione s-transferases, and risk for orofacial clefts.

Epidemiology. 2005 Sep; 16(5):698-701. [PubMed: 16135950].

21. Marazita, ML. Segregation analysis. In: Wyszynski, DF., editor. Cleft Lip and Palate: From Origin to Treatment. Oxford University Press; 2002. p. 222 233.

22. OMIM (Online Mendelian Inheritance in Man). 2009. available at

http://www3.ncbi.nlm.nih.gov/OMIM

23. Berk, NW.; Marazita, ML.. COSEs O Cret ip and palate: personal and societal implications. In: Wyszynski, DF., editor. Cleft lip and palate: from origin to treatment, New York: Oxford University Press; 2002. p. 458-46.

24. Omari F1, Al-Omari IK. Cleft lip and palate in Jordan: birtih prevalence rate. Cleft Palate Craniofac J. 2004 Nov;:41(6):609-12.

25. Campbell S, Lees C, Moscoso G, Hall P. Ultrasound antenatal diagnosis of cleft palate by a new technique: the 3D "reverse face" view. Ultrasound Obstet

Gynecol2005:25:12-18.

26. Cooper ME, Ratay JS, Marazita ML. Asian oral-facial cleft birth prevalence.

Cleft Palate Craniofac J. 2006 Sep:43(5):580-9.

27. Calzolari E, Pierini A, Astolfi G, Bianchi F, Neville AJ, Rivieri F. Associated anomalies in multi-malformed infants with cleft lip and palate: An epidemiologic study of nearly 6 million births in 23 EUROCAT registries. Am J Med Genet A. 2007 Mar 15;143A(6):528-37.

28. Katamara Rodriguesl; Marina Fermandes de Sena; Angelo Giuseppe Roncalli: Maria Angela Fernandes Ferreira. Prevalence of orofacial clefts and social factors in Brazil. Braz. oral res. vol.23 no.1 São Paulo Jan/Mar. 2009.

29. Mascarenhas, R., Ansari, T. Ornhodontic management of a cleft patient: A case report. Revista Latinoamericana de Ortodoncia y Odontopediatria Ortodoncia.ws edición electrónica julio 2011.

30. Oureshi WA, Beiraghi S, Leon-Salazar V. Dental anomalies associated with unilateral and bilateral cleft lip and palate. J Dent Child (Chic). 2012 May- Aug:79(2):69-73.

31. Altunhan H1, Annagür A, References Konak M. Ertugrul S. Ors R, Koç H. The incidence of congenitai anomalies associated with cleft palate/cleft lip and palate in neonates in the Konya region, Turkey. Br J Oral Maxillofac Surg. 2012 Sep:50(6):541-4 17

32. Buyu Y Manyama M, Chandika A, Gilyoma J. Orofaciai clefts at Bugando Medical Centre: associated factors and postsurgical complications. Cleft Palate Craniofac J. 2012 Nov;49(6):736-40

33. Collett BR1, Keich Cloonan Y, Speltz ML, Anderka M, Werler MM. Psychosocial functioning in children with and without orofacial ciefts and their

parents. Cleft Palate Craniofac J. 2012 Jul;49(4):397-405.

34. Josiane Souzal,; Salmo Raskin. Clinical and epidemiological study of orofacial clefts. J. Pediatr. (Rio J.) vol.89 no.2 Porto Alegre Mar/Apr. 2013

35. Kang SLI, Narayanan CS, Kelsall W. Mortality among infants born with

orofacial clefts in a single cleft network. Cleft Palate Craniofac J. 2012

Jul:49(4):508-11.

36. McGiattan K, ElIlis C. Team-oriented care for orofacial clefts: a review of the literature. Cleft Palate Craniofac J. 2013 Jan;50(1):13-8.

37. Tannure PN, Soares FM, Kuchler EC, Motta LG, Costa MC, Granjeiro JM,

Measuring the impact of quality of life of children treated for orofacial clefts: a

case-control study. J Clin Pedjatr Dent. 2013 Summer, 37(4):381-4

38. Ward JA, Vig KW, Firestone AR, Mercado A, da Fonseca M, Johnston W. Oral health related quality of life in children with orofacial clefts. Cleft Palate Craniofac J. 2013 Mar; 50(2):1 74-81.

39. Ling Sun, Wei Ran Li. References Cervical vertebral maturation of female children with Orofacial clefts. Cleft Palate Craniofac J. 2013 Sep:50(5).535-41. doi: 10.1597/11-215.

40. Ogunmuyiwa Stella Aimiede, Gboiahan Omoyosola Olalere, Olaosun Adedayo 03and Sotannde Adeshola. Orofacial Clefts: Our Experience in Two Suburban Health Facilities. Dentistry 2013:155. doi: 10.4172/2161-1122.!000155

41. Pius Agbenorku,Thomas Diby,Margaret Agbenorku,Fritz Abudc,Randy Sefenu,Daniel Osei, Mary Kofitse, Edem Maniwa. Orofacial Clefts: A Clinicai

Community Study in a Developing Country. SRN Plastic Surgery Volume 2013, Article ID 945254, 7 page http://dx.doi.org/10.5402/2013/945254

42. Figueiredo RF1, Figueiredo N, Feguri A, Bieski I, Mello R, Espinosa M,

Damazo AS. The role of the folic acid to the prevention of orofacial cieft: an

epidemiological study. Orai Dis. 2015 Mar;21 (2):240-7. doi: 10.1111/odi. 12256.

43. Soumi Samuel, B. Rajendra Prasad , Suchetha K.umari , S. Sandeep Tejaswi & Senal T.S. A clinical study of incidence and distribution and co- relating factors of cleft lip and cleft palate among karnataka & kerala population. NUJHS Vol.4, No.3, September 2014, ISSN 2249-7110.

44. Nagappan Nagappan,Joseph John. Soeiodemographic profile of orofacial cleft natients in India: A hospital-based study. International Journal of Medicine and Public Health, Jan-Mar 2015, Vol 5.1ssue 1.

45.Yin X, Zhang H, Zhu Z, Wang i, Du Y, Li S, Zhang Z, Fan w. Pan polymorphisms and non-syndromic orofacial cleft susceptibility in a Chinese Han population. Oral Dis. 2015 May,224):274-9. doi: i.111/odi.12435.

46. Jamile Sá , Luana Araújo, Lais Guimarıes. Samário Maranhão. Gabriela Lopes. Alena Medrado, Ri-cardo Coletta, Silvia Reis. Dental anomalies inside the cleft region in individuals with nonsyndromic cleft lip with or without cleft palate. Med Oral Patol Oral Cir Bucal. 2016 Jan 1:21 (1):e48-52.

47. lara Aparecida Zanon Andrade ,Sheila de Carvalho Stroppa,Juliana Yassue

Barbosa da Silva. Dental treatment of a child with oral cleft: a case report.

RSBO. 2015 Oct-Dec;12(4):377-82.

48. Omoroghogho Maria Izedonmwen, Claudia Cunningham, Tatiana V.

Macfarlane. What is the Risk of Having Offspring with Cleft Lip/Palate in Pre-

Matemal Obese/Overweight Women When Compared to Pre-Maternal Normal

Weight Women? A Systematic Review and Meta-Analysis. I Oral Maxillofac

Res. 2015 Jan-Mar, 6(1): el.

49. Kritika Jangid, Aurelian Jovita Alexander, Nadathur Doraiswamy Jayakumar, Sheeja Varghese, Pratibha Ramani. Ankyloglossia with cleft lip: A rare case report. J Indian Soc

Periodontol. 2015 Nov-Dec; 19(6): 690-693. doi: 10.4103/0972-124X.162207]

50. Vieira AR, de Carvalho FM, Johnson L, DeVos L, Swailes AL, Weber ML.

Deeley K. Fine Mapping of 6q23.1 ldentifies TULP4 as Contributing to Clefts.

Cleft Palate Craniofac J. 2015 Mar;$2(2):128-34. doi: 10.1597/ 13-023.

51. KS Ravichandral, KE VJayaprasad, A.A.K Vasa, S Suzan. A new techninue

impression making for an obrurator in cleft lip and palate patient. Journal of

Ludian Society of Pedodonues and reventive Dentistry, Vol. 28, No 4 Octol December, 2015, pp. 311-314.

52. Fernandes VM, Jorge PK, Carrara CF, Gomide MR, Machado MA, Oliveira TM. Three-dimensional digital evaluation of dental arches in infants with cleft lip and/or palate. Braz Dent J. 2015 May-Jun;26(3):297-302. doi: 10.1590/0105- 6440201300161.

53. Budarapu Silpa, P. Mahesh2, P. Srinivas Rao, K. Sahitha. Feeding Plate: A Boon to Cleft Palate Patients: A Case Report. Sch. J. Dent. Sci., 2016; 3(5):129 132.

54. Tonni G, Rosignoli L, Palmisano M, Sepulveda W. Early Detection of Cleft Lip by Three-Dimensiona! Transvaginal Ultrasound in Niche Mode in a Fetus with Trisomy 18 Diagnosed by Celocentesis. Cleft Palate Craniofac J. 2016

Nov: 53(6):745-748.

55. Cook AK, Kerins CA, Heppner CE. Dental Impacts on Health-related Quality of Life of Children with Orofacial Clefts. Pediatr Dent. 2016,38(3):218 23

56. Vesna Ambarkoval, Biljana Djipunova, Manu Batra, Siagana Trajkov. Oral

Rehabilitation of patient with Cleft Lip and Palate- A Case Report. J Dent Probl

Solut 4(4):061-065. Dol: http://doi.org/10. 17352/ 2394-8418.000051.

57. Giselle Firmino Torres de , Angelo Giuseppe. Orofacial clefts in Brazil and

Surgical rehabilitation under the Brazilan National Health System. Braz. oral

res., 2017, vol.31. ISSN 1806-8324. Anupriya Sharma, Naveen Sharma. Early prosthetic.

58. Suruchi Dogra, newbons with orofacial cleft using a feeding appliance: A case rehabilitation in newborms with cleftucim. report and review of literature. J Indian Acad Dent Spec Res 2017:5-11 715

59. Sanajay Kumar, Nimal Rajm AP, References Nivedita Pachore, Sudheer A, Lalitha Srivalli Prosthetic rehabilitation of the cleft palate patient with feeding plate: A Case report. American Joumal of Advances in Medical Science 2014: 244): 48-52.

60. Rajeev B R, Prasad K, Sihetty PJ, Preet R. The relationship between orofacial clefts and consanguineous marriages: A hospital register-based study in Dharwad, South India. J Cleft Lip Palate Craniofac Anomal [serial online) 2017 cited 2018 Nov 5]:4:3-8.

61. Alice V. Pereira, Nuno Fradinho, MD,* Sara Carmo, Juliana M. de Sousa, David Rasteiro, MD, Regina Duarte, Maria J. Leal. Associated Mal formations in Children with Orofacial Clefts in Portugal: A 31-Year Study. Plast Reconstr Surg Glob Open. 2018 Feb; 6(2): el635.

62. Bonsua AB, Dzomekua VM, Apiribua F, Asamoahb B, Mensahe KB Having a

child with orofacial cleft: Initial reaction and psychosocial experiences of

Ghanaian mothers. International Journal of Africa Nursing Sciences,Volume 8,

2018, Pages 132-140.

63. Intermational Perinatal Database of Typical Oral Clefts (IPDTOC) Working

Group. (2011). Prevalence at birth of cleft lip with or without cleft palate: Data

from the International Perinatal Database of Typical Oral Clefts (IPDTOC), 7he

Cleft Palate-Craniofacial Journal, 48, 66-81

64. World Health Organization. (2001, December). Global registry and database an craniofacial anomalies: Keport of a WHO registry meeting on craniofacial

anomalies. Bauru, Brazil: Author.

65. Tanaka, S. A.. Mahabir, R. G., Jupiter. D. C., & Menezes, J. M. (2012). Updating the epidemickogy of cleft lip with or without cleft palate. Plastic and

Reconstructive Surgery, 129, 511e-517e.

66. Parker, S. E., Mai, C. T., Canfield, M. A., Rickard, R., Wang. Y., Meyer. R. E. Corea, A. (2010). Updated national birth prevalence estimates for selected

birth defects in the United States, 2004-2006. Birth Defects Research Part A:

Clinical and Molecular Teratology, 88, 1008-1016.

67. Dixon, M. J., Marazita, M. L., Beaty, T. H., & Murray, J. C. (2011). Cleft lip and palate: Understanding genetic and environmental influences. Nature Reviews Genetics, 12, 167-178.

68. Mossey, P. A., Little. J., Munger, R. G., Dixon, M. J., & Shaw, W. C. (2009). Cleft lip and palate. The Lancet, 374, 1773-1785.

69. Cleft palate Foundation. Genetics and You, http://www.ciefline.org/docs/Booklets/GEN-01. Pdf

70. Barry L. Eppiey, John A. van Aalst, Ashley Robey,Robert J. Havlik, and A.

Michael Sadove. The Spectrum of Orofacial Clefting,

71. Vipawee Panamonta, Suteera Prad ubwong, Manat Panamonta, Bowornsiln

Chowchuen. Global Birth Prevaience ot Orotacial Clefts: A Systematic Review.

J Med Assoc Thai 2015; 98 (Suppl. 7): S11-S21 Jugessur, Jeffrey C. Murray. Genetics of

72. Fedik Rahimov,Astanand Nonsyndromic Orofacial Clefts. Cleft Palate-Craniofacial Jourmal, January 2012. Vol. 49 No. 1

73. P. Agbenorku. Orofacial Clefts: A Worldwide Review of the Problem. ISRN Plastic Surgery Volume 2013. Article ID 348465, 7

pages

74. Cleft Lip and Cleft Palate, http://www.medicinenet.com/ clett palate and cleft lip/article.htm.

75. IPDTOC Working Group (2011). Prevalence at birth of cleft lip with or without cleft palate. Data from the International Perinatal Database of Typical Oral Clefts (IPDTOC) Cleft Palate-Craniofac I 48:66-81

76. P.A. Mossey, W.C. Shaw, R.G. Munger, JC. Murray, J. Murnhy. and J. Little. Global Oral Health Inequalities: Challengesin the Prevention and Management of Orofacial Ciefts and Porential Solutions. Adv Dent Res 23(2):247-258, 2011

77. Mossey and Julian Little. Adóressing the challenges of clett lip and palate

research in India. Indian journal Piast Sur. 2009 Oct;42: $9- S18.

78. WHO. Reports, Human Genetics Programme Management of Noncommunicable Diseases: International Collaborative Research on

Craniofacial Anomalies. Ih: Mossey PA. Munger R, Murray JC. Shaw WC

editors, Global Strategies Towards Reducing the Health Care Burden of

Craniofacial Anomalies. Geneva: WHO; 2002. (ISBN 92 4 159038 6)

79. Inderbir Singh, GP Pal.Human Embryology 9th Edition: 2012

80. Jacobson S. Marcus E. Neuroanatomy IOr the Neuroscientist. Springer 2nd edition: 2011.

81. Melfi R. Aley K. Premar's Oral Embryology and Microscopic Anatomy.

Lippincott Williams & Wilkikins 10th edition: 2000

82. Samuel Berkowitz. Cleft Lip and Palate 2nd Edition:2006

83. P. Agbenorku. Orofacial Clefts: A Worldwide Review of the Problem. ISRN Plastic Surgery Volume 2013, Article ID 348465, 7 pages

84. Peter Mossey, Julian Little. Adóressing the challenges of cleft lip and Cleft

Palate research in India .Indian Journal of Plastic Surgery, Qct 2009, S9-S18

85. MurTay, J. C. Gene/environment causes of cieft lip and/or palate. Clin. Genet. 61: 248, 2002.

86. Gorlin, R. J., Cohen, M. M., Jr., and Levin, L. Orofacial clefting syndromes:

eneral aspects. In A. Motulsky, P. Harper, M. Bobrow, and C. Scriver (Eds.),

Syndromes of the Head and Neck. New York: Oxford University Press, 1990.

Pp. 697-698.

87. Mitchell, L. E., and Risch, N. Mode of inheritance of nonsyndromic cleft lip with or without palate: A reanalysis. Am. J. Hum. Genet. 51: 323, 1992.

88. Cohen, M. M., Jr., and Bankier, A. Syndrome delineation involving orofacial clefting. Cleft Palate Craniofac. J. 28: 119, 1991.

89. Stoil, C., Alembik, Y., Dot, B., and Roth, M. P. Associated malformations in cases with oral clefts. Cleft Palate Craniofac. J. 37: 41, 2000.

90. Vieira, A. R., and Oioli, 1. M. Canaidate genes for nonsyndromic cleft lip and palate. A.s.D.C. J. Dent. Child. 68: 272, 2001

91. P.A. Mossey, W.C. Shaw, R.G. Munger.J.C. Muray, J. Murthy, and J. Little.

Global Oral Health Inequalities: Chailenges in the Prevention and Management

of Orofacial Clefts and Potential Solutions. Adv Dent Res 23(2) 2011.

92. Prescott, N. J., Winter, R. M., and Malcolm, S. Nonsyndromic cleft lip and

palate: Complex genetics and environmental effects. Ann. Hum. Genet. 65: 505,

2001.

93. Wong FK, Hagg U. An update on the aetiology of orofacial clefts. Hong Kong Med J. 2004;10:331-6. Review. [PubMed:

15479962]

94. Singh D, Bastian TS, Kudva S, Singh MK, Sharma P. Classification Systems for Orofacial Clefts. Oral Maxillofac Pathol J 2015;6(1):556-560.

95. Syed Nasir Shah, Mariya Khalid, Muhammad Sartaj Khan. A REVIEW OF

CLASSIFICATION SYSTEMS FOR CLEFT LIPnAND PALATE PATIENTS-

96. S. A. Subramani, B. S. Murthy. A classification of cranio facio cervical

(branchial) clefts (Bangalore classification). Indiarn J Plast Surg July-December

2005 Vol 38 Issue 2

97. Fogh-Anderson P. Inheritance of hare lip and cleft palate. Copenhagen: Busck. 1942MORPHOLOGICAL CLASSIFICATIONS. JKCD June 2011, Vol. 1, No. 2

98. Kernahan DA, Stark RB. A new classification for cleft lip and palate. Plast Reconstructive Surgery.1958; 22:435-41

99. Pfeifer G. Schuchardt K(ed.). Treatment of patients with clefts of lips, alveolus and palate. Stuttgart: Thieme,1964, pp225-226.

100. Santiago A. Classification of cleft lip and palate for machine record coding. The Cleft Palate Journal Archive1969; 6(9): 434-9.JS.

101. Kernahan DA. Stark RB. A new classification for cleft lip and palate. Plastic and Reconstructive Surgery.1958, 22:435-41.

102. Millard DR (1976) Cleft Craft: the evolution of its surgery, vol 1. Boston: Liue Brown

103. Elsahy NI: The modified striped Y. A systemic classification for cleft lip and palate. Cleft lip and palate journal, 1973;10:247-250.

104. Kriens O. Lahshal: A concise documentation system for cleft lip, alveolus and palate diagnoses. In: Kriens 0, editor. What is Cleft Lip and Palate? A Multidisciplinary Update Workshop, Bremen 1987.Stuttgart: Thieme: 1989.

105. International Confederation for Plastic and Reconstructive Surgery, Cleft Palate Nomenclature. Newletter, Marclh 1968

106. Linton A., Whitaker, Hermine Pashayan, Joseph Reichman. A PROPOSED New Classification Of Carniofacial Anomalies. Cleft Palate Journal, July 1981, Vol 18 No.3

107. Harkins C, Berlin A, Harding K, LongaCre d, Snodgrasse R. A classification of le lip and cleft palate. Plastic and Keconstructive Surgery 1962: 29:31-9

108. Bender PL. Genetics of cleft lip and palate. J Pediat Nurs 2000 Dec;15(6):242-249 Elnassry. Classification of cleft lip and palate, Clinical Pediatric dentistry [online. Available from http://www.icyou.com/topics/medicalfields/ dental/ classification- cleft-lip palate-clinical-pediatric-dentistry+

109. Barry L. Eppley, D.M.D., John A. van Aalst, Ashley Robey, Robert J. Havlik, and A. Michael Sadove. The Spectrum of Orofacial Clefting. PLASTIC AND RECONSTRUCTIVE SURGERY, June 2005, Vol. 115, No. 7.

110. David, J. David; Moore, M.H; Cooter, R.D.; "Tessier Clefts Revisited With A Third Dimension," Cleft Palate Journal, July 1989, Vol. 26, No. 3, (163-185)

111. Tessier, P MD, "Classification of rare craniofacial clefts",Jounal of

Maxillofacial Surgery, 1976, Volume 4, pages 69-92: figures 1a, 1b.

112. Fogh-Anderson, P. Rare clefts of the face. Acta Chir. Scand. 129: 275. 1965. Martinot, V. L., Manouvrier, S. Anastassov, Y., Ribiere, J., and Pellerin, P. N. Orodigitofacial syndromes type I and II: Clinical and surgical studies. Cleft Palate Craniofac. J. 31:401, 1994,

113. Spolyar, J. L., Eldis, F, and Benjamins, D. Five cases of DeMyer sequence: An interophthalmic dysplasia. Cleft Palate Craniofac. J. 28: 103, 1991

114. Mulliken, J. B. Burvin, R., and Padwa, B. L. Binderoid complete cleft lip/palate, Plast. Reconstr. Surg. 111: 1000, 2003

115. Johnson, V. P., Swayze, V. W., I1, Sato, Y., and Andreasen, N. C. Fetal alcohol syndrome: Craniofacial and central nervous system manifestations. Am. J. Med. Genet. 61: 329, 1996.

116. Darzi, M. A.. and Chowdri, N. A. Oblique facial clefts: A report o

numbers 3,4, 5, and 9 clefts. Cleft Palate Craniofac. J. 30: 414, 1993.

117. Boo-Chai, K. The oblique facial cleft: A report of 2 cases with a review of 41 cases. Br.J. Plast. Surg. 23. 352, 1970.

118. Askar, I, Gurlek, A., and Sevin, K. Lateral facial clefts (macrosiomia). Ann. Plast. Surg. 47: 355, 2001

119. Poswillo, D. The pathogenesis of the first and second branchial arch syndrome. Oral Surg. 35: 302, 1973

120. Seyhan, T., and Kylynr, H. Median cleft of the lower lip: Report of two new cases and review of the literature. Ann. Otol. Rhinol. Laryngol. 11 1:217, 2002.

121. Irgebulem, L. M. Median cleft of the lower lip. Plast. Reconstr. Surg. 61: 787, 1978.

122. Millard, R. D., Jr., Lehman, J. A., Jr., Deane, M., and Garst, W. P. Median cleft of the lower lip and mandible. Br. J. Plast. Surg. 24: 391, 1971.

123. Pruzansky S. Description, classification, and analysis of unoperated clefts of the lip and palate. Am J Orthod. 1953; 39:590.

124. Fogh-Andersen P. Inheritance patterns tor cleft iip and palate. In: Pruzansky S, ed Congenital Anomalies or the Face and Associated Structures. Springfield, I CC Thomas; 1961:123-133. P. Inheritance of Harelip and Cleft Palate. Copenhagen,

125. Fogh-Andersen P, Inheritance of Harelip and Cleft Palate. Copenhagen,

Denmark: NytNordisk Forlag.Amold Busck; 1942.

126. Jaju R, Tate AR. The role of pediatric dentistry in multidisciplinary cleft palate teams at advanced pediatric dental residency programs. Pediatric Dent

2009;31 188- 92.

127. Udin RD. The pediatric dentist and the craniofacial anomalies team. Ear Nose Throat J 1986;65:305- 10

128. Hagerty RF. The role of the dentist on cleft palate teams. Birth Defects Orig Artic Ser 1980;16:111 4.

129. Goldberg WB, Ferguson FS, Miles RJ. Successful use of a feeding obturator for an infant with a cleft palate. Spec Care Dentist 1988,8:86- 9.

130. Fillies T, Homann C, Meyer U, Reich A, Joos U, Werkmeister R. Perioperative complications in infant cleft repair. Head Face Med 2007;3:9.

131. Jones JE, Henderson L, Avery DR. Use of a feeding obturator for infants with severe cleft lip and palate, Spec Care Dentjst 1982;2:116- 20.

132. Boros SJ, Reynolds JW. Ouodenai perforation: A complication of neonata!

nasojejunal feeding. J Pediatr 1974:85:107-8

133, Trenouth MJ. Campbell AN. Questionnaire evaluation of feeding methods for cleft lip and palate neonates. IntJ Paediatr Dent 1996;6:241- 4.

134, Grayson BH, Santiago PE, Brecht LE, Cutting CB. Presurgical nasoalveolar Tholding in infants with ciet p and palate. Cleft Palate Craniofac I

1999;36:486-9

135. Hanafy Eel- D, Ashebu SD, Naqeeb NA, Nanda HB. Pericardial sac perforation: A rare complication of neonatal nasogastric tube feeding. Pediatr Radiol 2006,36:1096- 8.

136. Clark DC. A review on fiuoride varnishes: An altermative topical fluoride

treatment. Community Dent Oral Epidemiol 1982;10:117- 23.

137. Crawford PJ. Sealant restorations (preventive resin restorations). An addition to the NHS armamentarum. Br Dent J 1988;165:250- 3.

138. Pitts NB, Kidd EA. The prescription and timing of bitewing radiography in the diagnosis and management of dental caries: Contemporary recommendations. Br Dent J 1992;172:225- 7..

139. Hali RK. Care of adolescents with cleft lip and palate: The role of the general dental practitioner. Int Dent J 1986; 36:120- 30.

140. E Ellis III, "Management of patients with orofacial clefts," in Contemporary Oral and Maxillofacial Surgery, pp. 623-645, Mosby,

St. Louis, Mo,USA, 4th edition, 2003.

141. Hayward JR: Cleft Lip and palate. in Hayward JR, editor: Oral surgery,

Springfield, IL, 1976, Charles C Thomas

142. Cohen MM. Syndromes with Cleft Lip and Cleft Palate. In Stewart, R. E.. and Prescott, G. H., editors, Oral Fac1al Genetics, St. Louis: The C.v. Mosby Co 1976.

143. Clementi M, Tenconi, R, Bianchi F, Stoli C, EUROSCAN study group.

Evaluation of prenatal diagnosis of cleft lip with or without cleft palate and cleft palate by ultrasound: experience from 20 European registries. Prenat Diagn 2000 20:870-875.

144. Christ JE,Meininger MG. Ultrasound diagnosis of cleft lip and cleft palate before birth. Plast Reconstruct Surg 1981;68:854.

145. Berge SJ, Plath H,Van De Vondel PT,Appel T, Nicderhagen B, Von Lindermid Reich RH, Hansmann M. Fetal cleft lip and palate: sonographic diagnosis. chromosomal abnormalities, associated anomalies and postnatal outcome in 70 fetuses. Ultrasound Obstet Gynecol 2001; 18:422-431.

146. Seeds JW, Cephalo RC. Technique of early sonographic diagnosis of bilateral cleft lip and palate. Obstet Gynecol 1983; 62:2S-7S.

147. Cohen MM, Bankier A. Syndrome delineation involving orofacial clefting. Cleft Palate J 1991; 28:19-120.

148. Nyberg DA, Sickler GK, Hegge FN, Kramer DJ, Kropp RJ. Fetal cleft lip with and without cleft palate: US classification and correlation with outcome. Radiology 1995; 195:677-684.

149. American Institute of Ultrasound in Medicine. Guidelines for performance of the antepartum obstetrical ultrasound examination. J Ultrasound Med 1996; 15:185- 187

150. Bronshteir M, Blumenfeld I. Kohn J. Blumenfeld Z. Detection of cleft lip by early second-irimester transvaginal sonography. Obstet Gynecol 1994; 84(1):73-76.

151. Cash C, Set P, Coleman N. The accuracy of antenatal ultrasound in the detection of facial clefts in a low-risk screening

population. Ultrasound Obstet Gynecol 2001: 18(5): 432-436.

152. Hafner E, Sterniste W, Scholler J, Schuchter K, Philipp K. Prenatal diagnosis or facial malformations. Prenatal Diagnosis 1997; 17(1):51-58.

153. Robinson JN, Mcllrath TF, Benson CB, Doubilet PM,Westgate MN,Holmes L,Lieberman E,Norwitz E.Prenatal ultrasonography and the diagnosis of fetal cleft lip. JUltrasound Med 2001; 20:1165-1170.

154. Chen ML, Chang CH,Yu CH, Cheng YC, Chang FM. Prenatal diagnosis of cleft palate by three-dimensional ultrasound. ULtrasound Med Biol 2001:27(8):1017- 1023

155. Chmait R, Pretorius D, Jones M, Hull A, James G, Nelson T. Moore T. Prenatal evaluation of facial cletts with tw0-dimensional and adjunctive three dimensional ultrasonography: a prospective trial. Am J Obstet Gynecol 2002;

87:946-949.

156. Saltzman DH, Benacerraf BR, Frigoletto FD.Diagnosis and management of fetal facial clefts. Am J Obstet Gynecol 1986; 155(2):377-379.

157. Benacerraf BR, Mulliken JB. Fetal cleft lip and palate: sonographic diagnosis and postnatal outcome. Plast Reconstr Surg 1993; 92(6):1045-1051.

158. Nicolaides KH. Salvesen DR. Saijder RJ. Gosden CM. Fetal facial defects:

associated malformations and chromosomal abnormalities. Fetal Diagn Ther

1993;8:1-9.

159. Vargervik K, Oberoi S. Hoffman WY. Team care for the patient with cleft

UCSF protocois and outcomes. J Craniofac Surg. 2009:20 Suppl 2:168-71.

160. Cassel CH, Daniels J, Meyer RE. Timeliness of primary cleft lip palate

surgery. Cleft Palate Craniofac J. 2009:46(6):588-97

161. Sullivan SR, et al. Palatoplasty outcomes in nonsyndromic patients with cleft palate: a 29-year assessment of one surgeon's experience. Craniofac Surg.

2009,20 Supp! 1:612-6.

162. Abbott MM, Kokorowski PJ, Meara JG. Timeliness of surgical care in children with special health care needs: delayed palate repair for publicly insured and minority children with cleft palate. J Pediatr Surg. 2011:46(7):1319 24

163. Santiago PE, et al. Reduced need for alveolar bone grafting by presurgical

orthopedics and primary gingivoperiosteopiasty. Cleft Palate Craniofac J. 1998:35(1):77-80..

164. Cutting C, et al. Presurgical columellar elongation and primary retrograde nasal reconstruction in one-stage Dilateral Clert lip and nose repair. Plast Reconstr Surg. 1998;101(3):630-9.

165. Cutting C, Grayson B, Brecht L. Columellar elongation in bilateral cleft lip. Plast Reconstr Surg. 1998;102(5):1 761-2 .

166. Gateno J, et al. A new Le Fort I internal distraction device in the treatment of severe maxillary hypoplasia. J Oral Maxillofac Surg. 2005;63(1):148-54.

167. Singh GD, Levy-Bercowski D, Santiago PE. Three-dimensional nasal changes following nasoalveolar molding in patients with unilateral cleft lip and palate: geometric rorphometrics. Cleft Palate Craniofac J. 2005:42(4):403-9

168. Spengler AL, et al. Presurgical nasoalveolar molding therapy for the treatment of bilateral cleft lip and palate: a preliminary study. Cleft Palate Craniofac J. 2006:43(3):321-8.

169. Ezzat CF, et al. Presurgical nasoalveolar molding therapy for the treatment of unilateral cleft lip and palate: a preliminary study. Cleft Palate Craniofac J.

2007;44(1):8-12.

170. Singh GD, et al. Three-dimensional facial morphology following surgical

repair of unilateral cleft lip and palate in patients after nasoalveolar molding. Orthod Craniofac Res. 2007;10(3):161-6.

171.Santiago PE, Schuster LA, Levy-Bercowski D. Management of the alveolar

cleft. Clin Plast Surg. 2014;41(2):219-32.

172. Maull DJ, et al. Long-term effects of nasoalveolar molding on three- dimensional nasal shape in unilateral clefts. Cleft Palate Craniofac J. 1999,36(5):391-7.

173. Grayson BH, Maull D Nasoalveolar molding for infants born with clefts of the lip, aveolus, and palate. Clin Plast Surg. 2004;31(2):149-58, vii

174. Da Silveira A.C, et al. Modified nasal alveolar molding appliance for

management of cleft lip defect. J Craniofac Surg. 2003;14(5):700-3.

175. Parapanisiou V, et al. Oral health status and behaviour of Greek patients with cleft lip and palate. Eur Arch Paediatr Dent. 2009;10(2):85-9.

176. Miller CK. Feeding issues and interventions in infants and children with clefts and craniofacial syndromes. Semin Speech Lang. 2011;32(2):1 15-26

177. Ramos-Gomez FJ, et al. Minimal intervention dentistry: part 3. Paediatric

dental care-prevention and management protocols using caries risk assessment

for infants and young children. Br Dent J. 2012;213(10):501-8

178. Crall JJ. Development and integration of oral health services for preschool-age children. Pediatr Dent. 2005:27(4):323-30.

179. Barbers BC, Rojas AC. Effects of combined toothbrushing and sweet diet limitation in dental caries prevention in a school setting after two-and-a-half years. J Philipp Dent Assoc. 1986;36(1):3-9.

180. Haring FN. Dental development in cleft and noncleft subjects. Angle Orthod. 1976:46(1):47--50.

181. Ribeiro LL, et al. Dental development of permanent lateral incisor in complete unilateral cleft lip and palate. Cleft Palate

Craniofac J. 2002:39(2):193-6.

182. Qureshi WA, Beiraghi S, on-Salazar V. Dental anomalies associated with

unilateral and bilateral cleft lip and palate. J Dent Child (Chic). 2012:79(2):69- 73.

183. Lucas VS, e al. Dental health indices and caries associated microflora in children with unilateral cleft lip and palate. Cleft Palate Craniofac J. 2000:37(5):447-52.

184. Johnsen DC, Dixon M. Dental caries of primary incisors in children with cleft lip and palate. Cleft Palate J. 1984;21(2):104-9.

185. Bokhout B, et al. Incidence of dental caries in the primary dentition in children with a cleft lip and/or palate. Caries Res. 1997,31(1):8-12.

186. Helms JA, Speidel TM, Denis KL. Effect of timing on long-term clinical

success of aiveolar cleft bone grafts. Am Orthod Dentofacial Orthop.

1987:92(3):232-40

187.Troxell JB, Fonseca RJ, Osbon DB. A retrospective study of aiveclar cieft

grafting.J Oral Maxiliofac Surg. 1982;40(11):721-5.

188. E 1Deeb M, et al. Can1ne eruption into grafted bone in maxillary alveoiar cleft defects. Cleft Palate J. 1982;19{1):9-16. Sharma S, et al.

189. Secondary alveolar bone grafting: radiographic and clinical evaluation. Ann Maxillofac Surg. 2012;2(1):41-5.

190. Nwoku AL. et al. Kerospective analys:s of secondary alveolar cleft grafts

1sing iliac of chin bone. Craniofac Surg. 2005;16(5):864-8.

191. Dewinter G, et al. Dental abnormalities, bone graft quality, and periodontal

conditions in patients with unilateral cleft lip and palate at different phases of

the odontic treatment. Cleft Palate CraniofacJ. 2003;40(4):343-50. 31

192. SernbG. RamstadT. The influence of alveolar bone grafting on the orthodontic and prosthodontic treatment of patients with cleft lip and paiate. Dent Update. 1999:26(2:60-4.

193. Rosen MS, Bzoch KR. The prosthetic speech appliance in rehabilitation of

patients with cleft paiate. I Am Dent Assoc. i958;57(2):203-10.

194. Tachimura T, Nohara K, Wada T. Effect of placement of a specech appliance on levator veli palatini muscle activity during speech. Cieft Palate Craniofac J. 200:37(5):478-82.

195. Raju H, Padmanabhan TV, Narayan A. Effect of a palatal lift prosthesis in

individuals with velopharyngeal incompetence. Int Prosthodont. 2909.2216):579-85.

196. Raj N, Raj V, Aeran H. Interim palatal ift prosthesis as a constituent of

multidisciplinary approach in the treatment of velopharyngea! incompetence. J

Adv Prosthodont. 2012:4(4):243-7.

197. Premkumar S. Clinical application of palatal lift appiance in veiopharyngeal incompetence. J Indian Soc Pedod Prev Dent. 2011;29(6 Suppl 2):S70-3.

198. Ross RB. Treatment variables affecting facial growth in complete unilateral cleft lip and palate. Cleft Palate J. 1987;24(1):5-77.

199. de Barros Ferreira Jr S, et al. survival of dental implants in the cleft area a -retrospective study. Cleft Palate Craniofac J. 2010;47(6):586-90.

200. Wermker ker KK,. et al. Dental implants in cleft lip, alveolus, and palate patients: a Systematic review. Int. Oral Maxillofac implants. 2014;29(2):384-90

201. Shah CP. Wong D. Management of children with cleft lip and palate, Can Med Assoc J. 1980;122(1):19-24

202. Lin FH, Wang TC. Prosthodontic rehabilitation for edentulous patients with palatal defect: report of two cases. J Formos Med Assoc. 2011:110(2):1204

203. Siow KK, et al. Satisfaction of orthognathic surgical patients in a Malaysian population. J Oral Sci. 2002:44(34):165-71.

204. Wolford LM, et al. Orthognathic surgery in the young cleft patient: preliminary study on subsequent faciai growth. J Oral Maxillofac Surg.

2008:66(12):2524 36.

205. Kumari P, et al. Stability of Cleft maxilla in Le Fort I Maxillary advancement. Ann Maxillofac Surg. 2013;3(2):13 43.

206. Bill J, et al. Orthognathic surgery in cleft patients. J Craniomaxillofac Surg. 2006;34 Suppl 2:77-81.

207. Waldron JM, et al. Cleft-affected children ir. Mayo: 1999-2067.J Ir Dent

Assoc. 2011;57(6):316-8.

208. Meazzini MC, et al. Long-term foilow-up of UCLP patients: surgical and

orthodontic burden of care during growth and final orthognathie surgery need.

Cleft Palate Craniofac J. 213 Jul 23. [Epub ahead of print].

209 Guvcn O0, et al. Surgical and prosthetic rehabilitation of edentulous adult cleft palate patients by gental implants. J Craniofac Surg. 2010;21(5):1538-41.

210. de Santis D, et al. Zygomatic and maxillary implants inserted by means of

computer-assisted surgery in a patient with a cleft palate. J Craniofac Surg.

2010;21(3):858-62

211. Guven O. Rehabilitation of severely atrophied mandible using free iliac crest bone grafts and dental implants: report of two cases. J Oral Implantol. 2007:33(3):122-6.

212. Laine J, et al. Rehabilitation of patients with congenital unrepaired cleft palate defects using free iliac crest bone grafts and dental implants. Int J Oral

Maxillofac Implants. 2002;17(4):573-80.

213. Pegelow M, Alqadi N, Karsten AL. The prevalence of various dental

characteristics in the primary and mixed dentition in patients 5bom with non

syndromic unilateral cleft lip with or without clet paiæte. Eur Orthod.

2012;34(5):561-70.

214. Kuijpers MA, et al. Incidental findings on cone beam computed tomography scens in cleft lip and palate patients. Clin Oral Iavestig. 2014;18(4):1237-44.

215. Devan MM. Biological demands of complete dentures. Am Dent Assoc.

1952;45(5):524-7.

216 Murthy J, Sendhilnathan S, Hussain SA. Speech outeome folloWing late

Dzimary palate repair. Cleft Palate Craniofac J. 2010:47(2):156-61.

217. Bridgeman JT, et ai. Comparison ot titanium and cobalt-chromittm

Atrial denture clasps. JProsthet Dent. 1997;:78(2):187-93.

218. Bartonova, et al. Long-term stability of prosthetic treatment otf oronasal and orcantral communications. Acta Chir Plast. 2005; 47(3):85-91.

219. Freitas JA, et ai. Rehabilitative treatment of cleft lip and palate: experience of the Hospitai for Rehabilitation of Craniofacial Anomalies/USP (HRACUSP) part 4: oral rehabilitation. J Appl Oral Sci. 2013,21(3):284-92.

220. Bidra AS. Esthetic and functionai rehabilitation of a bilaterai cleft palate

patient with fixed prosthodontic therapy. J Esthet Restor Dent. 2012:24(4):236 44.

221. Hochman N, et al. Functional and esthetic rehabilitation of an adolescent cleft lip cand palate patient. Quintessence int. 1991; 22(5):401-4

222. Krieger 0, et al. Failures and complications in patients with birth detecis restored with fixed dental prostheses and single crowns on teeth and/or implants. Clin Oral lImplants Res.

2099;20(8):809-16.

223.Pjetursson BE, Lang NP. Prosthetic treatment planning on the basis of

scientific evidence. J Oral Rehabil. 2008;35 Suppl 1:72-9.

224. K.aufiman FL. Managing the cleft lip and palate patient. Pediatr Clin Noth Am 1991:38(5):! 12747.

225. Kuttenberger J, Ohmer JN, Polska E. Initial counselling for cleft lip and palate: parents evaluation. needs and expectations. Int J Oral Maxillofac Surg. 201039(3):214-20.

226. Prebrahim N, et al. A comparison of tissue-engineered bone trom adiprsedenved stem cell with autogenous bone repair in maxillary alveolar cleft model in dogs. Int Oral maxillofac Surg. 2013:4205):562-8

227. Gimbel M, et al Repair of alveolar cleft defects: reduced morbidity with bone marrow stem cells in a resorbable matrix. J Craniofac Surg. 2007:18(4):895- 901.

228. Strauss RP. The organization and delivery ef cranio facial health services: the state of the art. Cleft Palate Craniofac J. 1999; 36(3):189-95

229. Matsuo A, et al. Osteogenic potential of cryopreserved human bone marrow-derived mesenchymal stem cells cultured with autologous serum. J Craniofac Surg. 2008;19(3):693-700.

230. M. M. Werler, C. Hayes, C. Louik., S. Shapiro. and A. A.Mitchell, "Multivitamin supplementation and risk of birth defects," American Journal of Epidemiologv. vol. 150. no. 7, pp. 675-682, 1999

231. P. D. Hodgkinson, S. Brown, D. Duncan et al., "Management of children with cleft lip and palate: a review describing the application of multidisciplinary team working in this condition based upon the experiences of a regional cleft lip end p .e centre in the United Kingdom," Fetal and Maternal Medicine Review, vol. 6, no. 1, pp. 1-27, 2005.

232. M. L. Speltz, G. C.Armsden, and S. S. Clarren, "Effects of craniofacial birth affects on maternal functioning pestinfancy. Journal of Pediatric Psychology. voi. 15, no. 2, pp. 177-1 96,0co

233. PS National Family and Health Survey;, india, 1992-93. Mumbai: International Institute for Population Sciences: 1995.

www.ingramcontent.com/pod-product-compliance
Ingram Content Group UK Ltd.
Pitfield, Milton Keynes, MK11 3LW, UK
UKHW022002190726
13853UKWH00004B/1690

9 798887 837741